MW01534690

The Teenager's Guide To Adulting Skills and Life Hacks

Learn The Practical, Social, and Communication Skills That Will Help Boost Your Self-Confidence, Manage Emotions, and Increase Independence

By Karen J. Conlon, LCSW

Copyright © 2023 by Karen J. Conlon, LCSW

All rights reserved.

Formatting provided by Trisha Fuentes

The content contained within this book may not be reproduced, duplicated, or transmitted without direct written permission from the author or the publisher.

Under no circumstances will any blame or legal responsibility be held against the publisher, or author, for any damages, reparation, or monetary loss due to the information contained within this book, either directly or indirectly.

Legal Notice:

This book is copyright protected. It is only for personal use. You cannot amend, distribute, sell, use, quote or paraphrase any part, or the content within this book, without the consent of the author or publisher.

Disclaimer Notice:

Please note the information contained within this document is for educational and entertainment purposes only. All effort has been executed to present accurate, up to date, reliable, complete information. No warranties of any kind are declared or implied. Readers acknowledge that the author is not engaged in the rendering of legal, financial, medical or professional advice. The content within this book has been derived from various sources. Please consult a licensed professional before attempting any techniques outlined in this book.

By reading this document, the reader agrees that under no circumstances is the author responsible for any losses, direct or indirect, that are incurred as a result of the use of the information contained within this document, including, but not limited to, errors, omissions, or inaccuracies.

ISBN: 979-8-9885367-0-3 (Paperback)
        979-8-9885367-1-0 (Hardcover)
        979-8-9885367-2-7 (Ebook)

To Nina, my bestie-boo and inspiration for all things good.

Contents

Chapter 1 - Why Life Skills For Teens Matter. 7

*I Am Literally a Teenager. Why Should I Even Care
About Life Skills?* *8*

What Is Adulting Anyway? *9*

Chapter 2- The Thrills and Spills of Being A Teen 13

The Unexpected Ups and Downs. *13*

Some Ways To Take Care Of Your Body and Mind *16*

**Chapter 3 - Understanding Your Emotions and
Communication Skills.** 27

Why Emotions Can Feel So Uncomfortable *27*

Daniel's Conflict Avoidance *31*

Stop and Reflect To Figure Out Your Feelings *33*

Dealing With Disappointment *37*

Jacob's Diamond Dreams. *38*

The Power of Choice. *39*

Six Tips for Dealing With Disappointment *41*

Talking to Moms, Dads or Guardians About Your Emotions. *44*

Seeking Out Other Support *48*

Chapter 4 - Self-Image Matters. 53

Kayla's Struggle With Herself. *54*

Dealing With Self-Esteem Issues *56*

How to Start Accepting Your Body *58*

Dealing with The Social Scene and Peer Pressure *60*

How Leah Got Her Cool Back. *62*

Tips For Managing Peer Pressure *67*

It's Okay to Ask For Help *69*

Chapter 5 - Chill Skills For Managing Your Anger 73

Ten Skills To Help You Chill. *74*

Chapter 6 - Critical Thinking Skills 79

What Critical Thinking Is And How It Can Help Teens *79*

Kaleb's College Confusions. *80*

Chapter 7 - Personal and Practical Safety Skills. 87

Personal Safety Skills *87*

Toxic Relationships: Recognizing Warning Signs *93*

Practical Safety Skills. *111*

Chapter 8 - Basic Daily Skills For A More Independent You 121

Time Management Skills: Manage Your Time Like A Pro!. *122*

Money Matters- It's Never Too Early To Budget and Save *124*

Marcus' Money Mishap *124*

Ways For Teens To Earn Money *125*

Become a Mini-Chef Overnight!. *128*

Easy Recipes at Your Fingertips. *129*

Conclusion - Final Pearls Of Wisdom. 135

References *138*

Image References. *142*

Introduction

"**Y**ou're going to be okay."

That is truly the one piece of advice I wanted to hear while growing up because that transition from tween to teen, from middle school to high school to college, is some adventure. It's like you're caught between two worlds, one which is slowly slipping away, and you don't know where to grab hold of or let go.

Don't get me wrong, I loved *most* of my teen years. It was a phase of my life filled with so much energy, hope, life, and beauty. The friendship bracelets my friends and I swore we would wear until we were old and gray. The Friday night slumber parties, the long nights making up our own dance moves, staying up later than we should've. I remember trying so hard to hold in our laughter in the middle of the night so our parents wouldn't realize we were still up. It was the *"They asked me not to tell anybody, but of course, I'm going to tell you"* moments with your besties, where you felt your heart beating with excitement at the tea you were about to spill. Those were arguably the best, most magnificent times of my life.

Then there were the messy parts and having to learn "the hard way" type of encounters. The heartbreaks from giving that special someone a piece of your heart, thinking they are "the one." The one who you are going to all the school dances with, and maybe even one day, to the same college. The one who you're going to figure out how to do this whole "life thing" with, but two weeks later, you find yourself heartbroken and crying in the school's bathroom because they told you that they don't want to be your person anymore. Wow, that hurt so deeply! Until that is, the next crush came along, and the butterflies in your stomach started up again. What a ride that was!

And, of course, who can forget about those devastating fights with your best friends without knowing exactly how you should even go about them? Do you ghost them, hoping they'll come around with a text message saying they're sorry and want you guys to patch things up?? Or maybe you needed to say sorry but were too embarrassed to face it or were afraid that you didn't have the right words. The friendship breakups and having to start all over again with new friends who were better aligned with who you are becoming and growing into. How do you approach these new friends? How do you start a conversation without being awkward and scaring them away?

Phew... It's a mess, a beautiful mess of self-discovery.

The best pieces of advice during these times of change came from my aunties. I am so glad I had them as role models for how to manage those difficult emotions during the hard times. That's not to say that my mom wasn't a role model for me, but she was my *mom*, so it was different, and I needed her in different ways than I needed my aunties. Still, having them all in my life was the biggest blessing ever; not everyone has those types of people to turn to when they're growing up, and that's why I want to start by sharing with you some wisdom they showered me with.

The first and most important thing I want to share is their philosophy on comparing myself to others. They told me that if I compared myself or wanted to be too much like others, I would never find out who I was or who I was meant to be. Now, that doesn't mean we don't have people we admire and strive to be like someday, but at the end of the day, we're better off celebrating our unique, individual traits and being the best we can be at any given time.

During my "rebellious" streak, my mom told me that the kind of people I kept around will be the ones who influence me the most; *"Show me who your friends are, and I'll tell you who you are,"* she used to say to me more often than I care to remember. ***Peer pressure is real, and that need to give in or fit in may always be there, but real friends are the ones who will never force you to do things that you don't want to do or are uncomfortable doing.*** The ones putting all the peer pressure are NOT the ones who will be there to take accountability or support you when you are getting in trouble for following their lead.

They taught me, too, that even as teens, we are more courageous than we take for granted. How often have you told yourself, "I can't!" simply because you don't think you're capable enough or are too worried about what your friends will say about you? During those times when I felt like I was their biggest letdown and disappointment, they taught me that mistakes are a normal part of the human experience. You WILL make many mistakes, but that doesn't make you any less of an imperfect human being than we are all meant to be. No one is perfect, and if we ***shoot for progress instead of perfection***, we're more likely to see our accomplishments. Still, sometimes the greatest lessons come from the hardest falls, and that's why growing up hurts so much sometimes.

We spend a lot of time telling ourselves how we can't do this and can't do that. I'm curious if you've taken any time to think about what you CAN do quite well, like being a good friend, a responsible pet owner, a reliable study partner, or just a good person. I bet you can probably think of at least one thing you are good at and are taking for granted.

For me, it was taking for granted that I was a good listener and always had good questions that made people reflect on things in ways that they had never considered. I took that for granted for SO long and instead, just focused on the things that I did not like about myself. I couldn't see that I was helpful by just being there to listen when a friend needed it. For a very long time, I took my "superpower" for granted, but guess what? Many years later, when I stopped taking it for granted and gave myself credit for what I was good at, I decided to go back to school and became a therapist. ♥

Please take a moment to think about the one thing you feel you do well, and when you choose what it is, pat yourself on the back and allow yourself to feel that well-earned pride!

There's no denying that at some point in your teen years, you'll yearn for more independence and want to have more say about what you do with your life. I get it because I've been there. But looking back now, I think about one of the best pieces of advice I ever received: ***"The best kind of growing up happens when you aren't trying so hard. Embrace this time and enjoy this phase of your life."***

I didn't think about it then, but this was excellent advice, and sometimes I wish that I had not rushed to grow up so quickly. There is so much time to be an adult with real adult responsibilities. Lucky for you, there's something called "adulting," and I've got plenty of good stuff tucked away within the pages of this book to help you get really good at adulting skills without missing out on being a teenager.

In this book, I will talk about the things that matter most to you right now and share some skills that will help you understand your feelings, manage your emotions and even make better decisions regarding friends and social situations. I'm talking about the real everyday issues and skills that will actually help, not the sounds-good-but-I-can't-put-it-to-use stuff that you find on social media, which is often unrealistic and difficult to put into practice.

I'll also talk about communication, conflict resolution and offer some ways to become more comfortable in social situations. As you read along, some topics we discuss will seem like impossible mountains to climb. Still, I want you to remember that you are not alone, even through the most challenging parts of it.

Let's get started and remember... I've got your back.

CHAPTER 1

Why Life Skills For Teens Matter

O kay, I know what you're thinking. Life skills? Ugh, sounds like one of those boring topics that put you to sleep faster than a lecture on the life of a rock. You may have gotten this book as a gift from a parent, guardian, or other adult in your life, and given how much the thought of learning about life skills measures up against spending time with your friends, I get that you may be a little reluctant to take time out of your busy day to read it. For that reason alone, I'm giving you some serious credit for even getting to this first Chapter.

Family, school life, culture, and your social environment are things that you are, to some degree, born into. Some life skills are picked up very naturally just by being in these different environments. Other life skills require more understanding of ourselves and need to be learned because they don't come naturally to most people, and this is what I will focus on with you. So now that you are here, I'm asking you for one favor: *Give this book a chance, and I promise to do my best to make it fun, helpful, and most importantly, relevant to you.*

I Am Literally a Teenager. Why Should I Even Care About Life Skills?

That's truly a great question and an excellent place to start talking about why life skills would matter to you, even in the early stage of life that you're in. Developing good, basic life skills is like having a secret stash of knowledge that, when used consistently and often, will undoubtedly make a huge difference in your daily life.

Learning foundational life skills as a teen will absolutely help boost your confidence and self-esteem for years to come. Whether it's cooking a meal for yourself, acing a school project, or just being able to communicate what you're feeling in a way that makes you feel good, learning how to do these things well will always leave you feeling good about yourself.

Better decision-making = making better choices. Most of your decisions are probably centered around who to hang out with, how you want to be seen, and how to spend your free time. Life skills also mean learning decision-making skills that help you feel empowered to make better choices or just being able to think about things differently than before. Each small victory adds up and will help you feel even more confident about navigating the ups and downs of being a teen. As you grow up, the decisions that you need to make will get bigger and have more impact on your life, so having a good life skills foundation early on will set you up to be a better thinker and make choices that match what you want in life—with much less anxiety.

Let's talk about independence. I'm stating the obvious here when I say that you're getting closer to being an adult-there's no going back now, so having some solid life skills is your ticket to gaining more independence now versus later. When you learn how to manage your time, think things through rationally and thoughtfully, set goals, and handle everyday tasks well, you also become more self-assured and self-reliant, all of which are great qualities to have in preparation for the day you take off to college, live alone or with roommates. But that's all a bit in the future, so for now, let's focus on the fact that having life skills at your age can help you show the people who are likely to have the most influence in this area (your parents/guardians) that you are trustworthy, reliable, and responsible. In other words, it is a way to build their trust in you. Not a bad thing to have!

I can go on and on about why learning life skills is such a fantastic plus for you now, but I'll stop gushing about it and trust that you've gotten the point. I hope this has helped you become more interested in the power that learning different life skills can give you. As you learn to make better choices, build strong relationships, and gain independence, you will find that the doors to many awesome opportunities will begin and continue to open for you. Believe me when I tell you, start learning them now, and it will be a game changer.

What Is Adulting Anyway?

So, let's get on with defining and getting into what adulting is...

Growing up, or "adulting," is like taking off on an exciting, big adventure, and yes, it might seem like a lot at first. There are so many new responsibilities that come with adulting that it can sometimes feel like you're carrying an overstuffed backpack filled with stuff you would prefer to dump out and ignore.

To me, adulting is that weird place and stage in your life where you get really excited about growing up and becoming independent but also want to still enjoy the benefits of being "a kid."

It's that point in your life where you have to learn to stand on your own two feet but still feel the need for an adult to have your back and catch you if you fall.

It's learning to care for your body by making healthier choices when the easier, no-so-healthy option is staring you in the face.

It's learning how to manage your allowance or paycheck and how to do your laundry so you don't have to wait for laundry day to wear your favorite t-shirt.

It's about learning how to manage the waves of emotions you experience daily and resolving conflict with some really good talks.

In the following few chapters, we will look at some of the skills that would be most helpful for you to consider while you're practicing adulting. But this journey isn't just about tasks and jobs; it's a lot about emotions, too! Making big decisions about your life comes with many feelings, and owning up to your choices can feel as exhilarating as a rollercoaster ride. Yes, it might seem a little scary at times. Sure, there might be moments when you feel alone or overwhelmed.

Even the greatest adventurers in history started with "not knowing," and I'm betting they sometimes felt that way, too. Still, it's also incredibly empowering because it allows you to show the world just how capable you are. Remember that with each step you take, you're not only finding your place in the world, but you're also creating it.

And the best part about adulting? It's your personal journey of self-discovery. You'll learn more about who you are and what you genuinely love. You'll also realize that some things you thought you liked aren't for you anymore. It's all part of the adventure and makes the journey even more exciting.

Growing up isn't just about tackling challenges; it's about celebrating accomplishments—big and small. With every new day, you're becoming a stronger, wiser, and more incredible version of yourself. Embrace the journey, and remember, you're creating your own amazing story every step you take.

You've totally got this!

Think About It...

Reflection is an important part of learning something new and making it stick. At the end of each Chapter, we'll take some time to reflect on what you feel you've learned or may want to think about further. I'll ask you some questions to help you review what we've covered and think about how to start practicing the skills discussed throughout the Chapter. I encourage you to write your answers on the "MY THOUGHTS" page I've included after this section in each chapter or use whatever method works best for you.

1. What do you think about when you hear the word "adulting"?

2. Make a list of the top 3 skills you feel would be most helpful for you right now.

3. From your list, are there any skills that intimidate you? If so, why?

MY THOUGHTS

CHAPTER 2

The Thrills and Spills of Being A Teen

The Unexpected Ups and Downs

Have you ever sat on a roller coaster, feeling a flurry of different emotions all at once? Excitement, fear, curiosity, and the nervous energy that fills you until you think you might burst? Well, this is pretty close to what it can feel like to be a teenager on any given day. It can be the most unpredictable ride, filled with changes, joys, pressures, and intense emotions. Keeping up with school grades and pursuing your hobbies, interests, or extracurricular activities. And, of course, there's the excitement and confusion of navigating your first crushes, which is a rollercoaster of its own...

Standing in front of your mirror can be confusing, too, as you notice how your body changes, sometimes feeling strange or uncomfortable. Some days, you feel good about yourself, and the next day, you can't figure out why none of the clothes you have picked out seem to be working. For me, it was the unexpected breakouts, ugh! I remember worrying about the acne that seemed to pop up overnight and feeling like there was not much I could do other than ride it out.

The issues you face in your teen years aren't just about growing taller or dealing with acne—the real kicker is the emotional stuff happening inside. You're not a kid anymore, but not quite an adult, either. It's a strange and sometimes scary middle ground, filled with new feelings and thoughts you're trying to understand. You're trying to figure out who you are, what you want, and where you fit in this big, complex world.

The landscape of friendships can be ever-changing, too! One day, you and your bestie are cracking up over inside jokes. Then, suddenly and without warning, they are part of a different crowd, leaving you feeling like an outsider. When I was 15 years old, I went through a situation that was very much like what I just described. My best friend accused me of liking her boyfriend, which was so untrue! I tried to ask her where she was getting this from or why she was even thinking that. She didn't have an answer for me and just gave me the cold shoulder. I remember that day like it was yesterday because it left me feeling so bad about myself and confused about what had changed. Most of all, it was hard to understand why or how such a close friendship could change so quickly without an explanation.

Those were the moments of loneliness when I felt like I was the only one who didn't understand and drifted off into a sea of anxiety and uncertainty. I eventually learned that, given the situation, my feelings were completely valid and normal. We all have moments when we don't know what to do or how to feel, and sometimes, the hardest part is to sit with the uncertainty. It happens to you, to your friends, and to every single person on this planet, whether they admit it or not.

Then, there are those secret dreams that you wouldn't dare think of sharing, not even with your bestie. Okay, this might be a good time to fess up on mine. When alone in my room, I would imagine myself being a famous singer and actress, shining brightly on stage, hitting every high note with zero effort... I'm talking Adele status here. In my pretend world, I was big time! I would sing into my pretend microphone (which was typically one of my favorite hairbrushes) and put on performances for my pretend audience. The roar of the crowd when I hit those high notes was unbelievable!

To answer the question you may now be asking yourself: YES, I knew I was only singing to myself in front of my dresser mirror. But allowing myself to have those big, outrageous, larger-than-life dreams felt thrilling and fun back then! These were very private dreams that I kept to myself, and even though I never became a famous performer (admittedly, I actually have zero singing skills), imagining myself in front of that huge audience helped me feel confident about being able to speak in front of crowds, a skill that has ultimately helped me both in school and in my professional life.

The reality is that being a teenager means you have the power to be creative and dream big, which is a beautiful thing! Those big dreams are often the most excellent sources of inspiration and motivation; they can even be the things that get us through our most challenging times. **Consider this for a moment: your bicycle, your television, smartphones—all of these things started with a dream many people didn't believe in, laughed at, or scoffed at.** But big dreams inspire us to be persistent and creative and give us the courage to overcome obstacles. So remember to dream big—you never know where it will lead you.

Some Ways To Take Care Of Your Body and Mind

Let's switch gears here and talk a bit about navigating this big old rollercoaster when you are a teen with limited resources. If you're anything like I was when I was your age, you either don't have the money, time, or permission to buy things that you think may help you feel better, so what's a young person to do? I'll share some things that helped me and often still do.

Loving Yourself Through Self-Care

The first thing that I think about is doing the little things that helped to calm my body and mind. Simple things, like the magic of a warm shower. After a long day at school or after-school activity, one of my favorite things would be to stand in the shower and let the warm water hit my neck. As the drops of water reached my shoulders, I imagined that they were washing my worries away, and a feeling of relaxation would begin to take over. This was a real source of relaxation for me, and just visualizing that my worries were getting washed away really left me feeling calmer. The downside of this, of course, was when there was no hot water left for my family and their baths... ooops! But even their complaining couldn't take away the feeling of calm that I felt.

I also started to take closer care of my hygiene, asking my mom to help me look for a different deodorant if I noticed that the one I was using wasn't working as well as before (hormonal changes happen for everyone and can change the effectiveness of deodorant) or brushing my teeth at night, even for 30 seconds. If my face started to break out more than usual, I would ask my mom to help me look for a face wash for more sensitive skin.

I made sure to wash my hair and condition it because my curls needed some extra moisture and tender-loving care. And while I really loved to pile my clothes on my desk chair (yes, I had a hamper, but I preferred to drop them on the chair), I would sometimes give into my mother's frustrations about the state of my room and go into a full-on disaster-area, clean-up mode. And you know what? As much as I didn't want to admit it, seeing my room in such an organized and clean state really made a difference! I realized that I felt really good when I did these things for myself because, ultimately, these small acts were ways of showing love to myself.

On the face of it, these seemingly small acts might not appear as things that would help you feel better or even be considered life skills, but they actually are because "life skills" aren't always about the huge things that we accomplish for others to take notice of. These small acts are also guides you are creating on how to care for your mind and body, helping you recognize what you need and understand what feels right for you, regardless of what anyone else is doing. They are acts of kindness to and for yourself that will also help you become more self-aware and even help you develop empathy towards others because it's easier to be kind to others when we are kind to ourselves.

Being kind to ourselves helps us see things from other people's points of view and better connect with others. It reminds us that everyone, including us, is trying their best with what they have. It helps us to feel better about who we are, which means we are less likely to feel insecure or compare ourselves to others negatively. Instead, we can focus on being more understanding and caring towards them. In summary, there's really no downside to loving yourself through self-care. How are you practicing self-care and self-kindness? If you're not doing so yet, this might be a great time to start.

Practicing Self-Kindness With Positive Affirmations

Have you ever heard of affirmations? I'm sure that some of you probably have. Positive affirmations are like pep talks you give yourself, used to help remind you of things you want to do, motivation, or even self-encouragement in one or two short sentences. An affirmation might also describe a mindset you want to adopt or a behavior you strive to develop.

When I was a teenager, "affirmations" were not a thing, but if I think back on what worked in similar ways, it would have to be lyrics from my favorite songs. And that's the beauty of affirmations—they can come from whatever source you want.

Reading a positive affirmation you've picked out for yourself is a great way to start your day. It can also give you the little boost of confidence that you might need or be a nice ending to the evening. It sounds simplistic, but saying these affirmations to yourself on a regular basis can help you believe in yourself and your abilities. And again, no fluff here! There is actual scientific evidence that affirmations have a positive impact on your brain function, mindset, and how positively you see yourself. What an amazing concept! The thought that saying something positive to yourself on a daily basis can actually make beneficial changes in your brain??

My current favorite affirmation is *"I am braver than I believe, stronger than I seem, and smarter than I think."* This affirmation has become my daily reminder that I can face any challenge that comes my way, even when I'm not feeling so brave or self-confident. You may also find some comfort in those kind words that affirmations can offer you—here are a few to try on for size:

1. "I am strong, even when I feel weak."

2. "I am loved, even when I feel alone."

3. "I am good at (playing the guitar, painting, running, etc.) and will continue to grow."

4. "I am a good brother/sister/friend, and my love makes a difference."

5. "I have a great sense of humor that brings joy to others."

6. "I am sensitive to others' feelings, and this empathy makes me kind."

7. "Every challenge I face helps me grow stronger."

8. "I am brave enough to face my fears."

9. "My worth is not defined by my mistakes."

10. "I am always enough."

Does any one of these speak to you? I'm going to invite you to try it yourself. Choose one of those listed here, or find one on your own and say it to yourself daily for an entire week. And remember that it can come from a song, a book, whoever or whatever inspires you! See what happens. Maybe nothing happens, but maybe... just maybe... something really good does.

Using Movement To Release Anxiety

As a young child and teen, I struggled with a bit of hyperactivity. In class, it was difficult for me to concentrate on a subject if I did not find that particular topic interesting. I would start to fidget, tap my foot, or try to talk to my friends, none of which—as you can imagine—went over well with the teachers. My difficulty concentrating would quickly turn into anxiety, so much so that my stomach would hurt.

At some point, I realized that sitting in the classroom for such long periods would further increase my anxiety. So, when I went home after school, I started using movement to let out my anxious energy. My favorite go-to activity was to dance like crazy to my favorite tunes, feeling the rhythm to shake off anxiety.

On other days, I would take walks with my next-door neighbor, who was also my age, or I would ask her to let me know when she was going out to walk her dog so I could accompany her. Having her dog around was extra helpful because we could play fetch and run around without worrying about looking silly.

Movement can be a powerful outlet to release all of your anxious energy. Whether going for a run, shooting some hoops, dancing to your favorite playlist, or even sitting while doing some light weightlifting reps, these are all activities that can help you clear your mind, pent-up energy, and stress. I'm pretty sure that you can come up with a list for yourself, but hey, I'm writing a book on all this stuff, so I couldn't help but come up with a list of low, moderate, and high-intensity movements for you to consider:

- Simple stretching exercises to help release muscle tension

- Slow, leisurely walks, taking in the sights, sounds and scents around you

- Dancing to your favorite pop or rock songs (because you are a rock star, yaaasss!)

- Jumping rope—slow, moderate, or fast, whatever feels good to you

- Fast-paced walking, getting the heart rate up just a bit

- Sprinting, or if you're up for it, going for a run

- Playing a sport or just throwing the ball around with a friend

There were times, however, when my difficulty with concentration was connected to not getting enough sleep. When I was a teen, I didn't have a smartphone, but I did have a TV in my bedroom, and it kept me up at night. I noticed that I developed a habit of turning the TV on to try to sleep, but that only resulted in me feeling more wired, or worse, more tired AND unable to sleep. By the time I did fall asleep, it was in the middle of the night and out of sheer exhaustion. You can imagine how awful I felt the next day: groggy, irritable, and oh, so tired. Sometimes, it was all of that plus a good dose of anxiety to top it off. Ugggh!

It wasn't until a bit later in life that I learned about the connection between sleep, the developing teenage body, and how teenagers actually need much more sleep than adults. Now, I know that some days, it just feels like staying up all night and FaceTimeing with your best friends is all you want to do. If that's not an option, binge-watching your current Netflix series is a close second best because who wants to wait until tomorrow to watch what happens in that next episode?

I would be a complete hypocrite if I said that binging on my favorite series is not something I do. Sometimes, I know I will pay the price for staying up late the next day, and I will confess that it has been worth it on a couple of occasions. But mostly, they haven't been, and I always regret how tired and unfocused I feel the next day. Teens struggling with sleep deprivation is a real thing, and there's been A LOT of research on it. But before I go on, I'm going to take a minute to discuss FOMO.

When FOMO Messes With Your Sleep

If you're not familiar with what the abbreviation "FOMO" means, it stands for "Fear Of Missing Out." It's like that feeling you get when you're worried about missing out on fun things your friends might be doing without you. This feeling can really mess with your sleep, especially when it feels like everyone is constantly posting something on socials, and you feel the need to stay on top of it all.

FOMO is usually the culprit for teens staying up super late, chatting, and checking their social media because they don't want to miss anything. Seeing exciting or stressful posts (like friends at a party you weren't invited to) can make your brain super active, making it hard to relax and fall asleep. These feelings can also make you feel bad or stressed and do not leave you in a good state to prepare for a restful night's sleep.

Screens from phones or computers give off what is called blue light. Blue light messes with a sleep hormone in our body called melatonin. Melatonin is our body's natural alarm clock that tells us when it's time to sleep. So, when blue light from our devices reduces our melatonin production, it's harder for us to fall asleep and get a good night's rest. It's like our body gets tricked into thinking it's still daytime.

When you're so focused on making sure that you don't miss anything before the lights go out, it is challenging to keep a regular bedtime, which your body's internal clock really needs. So, as you can see, FOMO can get in the way of getting a good night's rest in many different ways.

And at the end of the day, what are you really missing out on? Anything posted that evening will likely still be there the next day, and if it's really newsworthy, you will know about it. So ask yourself, is FOMO really worth losing sleep over?

If reading all of this has made you re-think your bedtime routine, and you're interested in trying to get better sleep so that you can wake up feeling refreshed and energized, I'll share some quick tips to get you started on a good sleep routine:

- **Do relaxing things to help you wind down in the evening.** This could mean taking a soothing bath, listening to calming music, or reading a few pages of a book. Important note to all my bookworms: this suggestion can be precarious because one minute you're telling yourself, "Just one more page…" and the next thing you know, it's 3:00 a.m., and you're five chapters in too deep. My advice to you is to set a timer for yourself and put the book down when it goes off.

- **Make your bedroom a soothing sanctuary.** One way to do this is by making sure your bedroom is tidy before laying your head down that evening. If you like a fluffy pillow, get some for your bed and scatter them around. If you don't mind scents, lavender is known to help with relaxation, so a little drop of light-scented lavender spray on your pillows and sheets will help set the stage for a more relaxing night of sleep.

- **Go to bed at the same time each evening.** This is a hard one, even for me. Still, when you practice this consistently, your body's internal clock (a.k.a "circadian rhythm") will naturally get used to sleeping at a specific time. You'll also be less tempted or able to pull those late-nighters.

- **Make your evenings a time for mindfulness.** The blue light our screens put out is often the biggest cause of poor or disturbed sleep cycles. Apart from the blue light they emit, you may also feel more compelled to text your friends or get distracted by Googling things that, in the grand scheme of things, aren't all that important. When you realize that you are starting to go down this rabbit hole, see if you can remind yourself that you still have tomorrow or the day after to do that. For now, try turning off the phone or computer and see how it goes for you.

- **Avoid having caffeine or sugary drinks before bed.**
  Caffeine + Sugar = Jitters. Need I say more?

Think About It...

You made it to the end of this chapter, and I'm celebrating you for it! You may be feeling overwhelmed because this was a lot of info to take in. So, please take a moment to catch your breath, and once you've regathered your thoughts, use these questions to guide you in reflecting on everything we've learned!

1. What changes are you noticing as you navigate your teen years? Are you feeling the pressures of so many changes, or are you riding the wave without many bumps along the way? What kinds of things would help make things easier for you?

2. Try out one or two self-care rituals this chapter notes for 7 days straight. It may be making your bed every day or taking a warm shower before bed. Be intentional and check in with yourself on how you feel after you do it. Do you somehow feel better (physically better or emotionally)? If so, keep it going until it becomes a daily routine.

3. Positive affirmations are a simple but powerful tool that can come from any source you want. Do you have a favorite quote or a favorite song that inspires you to feel good about yourself? Go ahead and use that as your daily affirmation and repeat it to yourself on a daily basis. You will eventually begin to feel the positive effects of how you are speaking to yourself.

MY THOUGHTS

Understanding Your Emotions and Communication Skills

Why Emotions Can Feel So Uncomfortable

Another piece of advice that I heard time and time again while growing up was this: "Communication is key if you want to thrive and succeed in life." But when you're a kid, who the heck even knows what that means! Still, years later, many of the people who come to me for help want to learn how to become a better communicator, so there must be something to this advice, right? The truth is that learning how to communicate takes patience and practice, but most of us think that some people are just born with it, as if it was a trait that we inherit. Well, it isn't something that we inherit, which is really good news because it means that anyone can learn how to be a good communicator.

For many of us, communicating can be hard. Why is it such a struggle to open up and talk about what bothers us, or about how we feel? I'll tell you what the struggle was for me: **FEAR**. It was the fear of being judged and labeled as a social outcast for being too different, too much, or too little of anything. The thing about being a teenager is that you tend to think that everyone else besides you is normal. As a result, you may end up downplaying your own feelings to make room for other people's feelings.

The other big reason why we don't often feel comfortable talking about our emotions is because we tend to think that no one else will understand. When you look at your teachers and your parents, it's easy to forget that they went through the same phase in life you are in. They go to work every day, they have relationships, they problem-solve, and oftentimes, they are also helping you. So talking to them would be pointless because what would they know about what's going on in your internal world, right? But let me tell you that eventhough they did grow up in a different time with a different set of rules, there's actually quite a lot that you can learn from us ancient ones.

Let's be honest- putting yourself "out there" can be seriously terrifying. It's like standing on a stage in front of an audience and sharing your talent for the very first time with a group of people, not knowing how they will react or if they will get what you're trying to say. Sometimes, talking about emotions isn't encouraged in our homes, making it harder to talk about them to anyone. I've known wonderful families and parents with the best intentions who only encourage expressions of happy or pleasant emotions. You might ask yourself why this isn't necessarily a good thing, and I'll tell you why.

We have a range of different and varying emotions for a reason. Emotions are a signal to us about how we feel regarding anything we might be experiencing, and they often tell us something about a situation. When we are only tuned into specific types of emotions (for example, happy, happy, joy, joy!), we are training our brains and bodies to push down other essential emotions, such as anger, irritability, confusion, and sadness, to name a few. Many times, these are considered to be "negative emotions." In many households, we get the message that expressing those types of emotions makes you weak or that expressing those types of emotions is strictly taboo.

Speaking as a parent, I can tell you that yours are parenting you in the best way they know, often taking from what they learned from their parents, and nobody is perfect. They may have learned that expressing emotions, especially ones that may make others uncomfortable, is a bad thing. As parents, we often pass down what we have learned from our own parents, and what you will learn as you grow up is that a lot of times, we are right, and a lot of times, we are wrong. And that's okay, too, because the opportunity to learn some ways of doing things differently is always there.

Here's a little reflection exercise for you. Read the following sentences and consider how comfortable or free you would feel to say them out loud to someone:

- *I'm not sure how to feel, but I am not okay.*
- *I don't know how to cope with this.*
- *There are things that I am struggling to deal with.*
- *I need someone to talk to.*
- *I wanted to say sorry, but I was embarrassed.*

We don't always have the strength or the vocabulary to say the things we feel out loud because we are so often shamed into believing that there's something wrong with us if we do. This is especially true when we assume that our emotions are supposed to make sense. Emotions do not always make sense because they are not always logical. They are not like math problems or data that can be put on a spreadsheet. They aren't always rooted in logic because we are human beings with lots of experiences and memories that make up who we are. All of those things can factor into how we feel. And that is OKAY.

Sometimes, we aren't even clear on what we are feeling, but our bodies tell us that something is wrong or right. Think about the last time you had butterflies in your stomach at the thought of meeting up with your besties for an amazing day of fun that you had planned for a while. On the other hand, think about the last time you experienced feeling nauseous or even got a stomach ache before a big test, regardless of how much studying you've done.

Emotions just want to exist as they come to us. They want us to learn to accept them as they come. That being said, there are some emotions, like overwhelm, which, if left unaddressed, can develop into hard-to-manage anxiety and lots of stress on your physical body and mind.

You are not just the future, dear friend. You are the present, and if I can help you learn how to manage some of your emotions sooner rather than later, you will be in a much better position to express them more freely as you grow up. Let's continue on with more exploration of how emotions influence our behavior, and how to identify what it is that we are truly feeling.

¹Daniel's Conflict Avoidance

I want to introduce you to a friend named Daniel. Daniel is 16 years old, and lately, he's finding that he's having a tough time facing anything that he considers "conflict." In addition, he recently experienced his very first romantic break-up, and dealing with not-so-easy emotions like sadness, anger, and heartbreak has made him want to avoid conflict even more.

Daniel has grown to dislike conflict so much that he will do almost anything to avoid it. He would much rather spend his time scrolling his favorite social media app and watching funny reels so that he doesn't have to think about the discomfort his emotions are causing him. And who can blame him, right? After all, laughter is a kind of therapy on its own, so funny videos with people doing the most ridiculous antics here and there should do the trick. Still, the problem is that when the funny videos start getting boring and scrolling down starts getting old, Daniel is still left feeling all those emotions that he's trying to avoid because those outlets don't give him what he really needs, which is to be able to express his feelings and thoughts.

By keeping those bottled up, Daniel's thoughts and feelings keep building up inside like grime in a clogged pipe: On the outside, everything might look and seem to be working perfectly, but as the line gets even more congested, one day at a completely unexpected moment, the pipe explodes. So if Daniel's heart is "the pipe" and his emotions are the residue clogging the drain, think about what will happen when his heart can't carry that load of pressure anymore. When he decides that continuing to feel this way is not okay, but doesn't have

---

1   "The vignettes in this book are a compilation of the author's subjective and objective experiences. Any names, characters, events or incidents, are fictitious. Any resemblance to actual persons, living or dead, or actual events is purely coincidental."

the tools (or words) to clear out his pipes, he may find himself reacting in any number of ways that ultimately make him feel even worse.

For example, Daniel may struggle to focus and find that his grades have begun to suffer. He may also get very angry or annoyed at things that don't deserve that big of a reaction. Daniel may even start to keep more to himself, feeling ashamed that he doesn't know what to do about his emotions and not wanting to let anyone know he could use some support.

Like breathing, emotions are a natural part of existing, and they are something that we all experience. On the good days, you'll feel like the stars have perfectly aligned themselves and are rooting for you. On the not-so-great days, all you may want and wish for is to be left alone. Those days can get pretty rough, especially when you don't understand why you're feeling the way you do. Emotions can be downright confusing, but even in those moments, we have to learn the sweet art of "accepting, not rejecting" what we're feeling. And what does "accepting, not rejecting" look like?

- You can start by accepting that your emotions are real, valid, and worthy of taking up space.

- You don't have to pretend that your feelings aren't there—they're there for a reason, and there's something that they're trying to tell you.

- You don't have to sweep your emotions under the rug and pretend that something/someone didn't bother or upset you because, again, your feelings matter and deserve a voice.

- It can also be very fulfilling to learn from your emotions by sharing them with someone you trust and allowing them to support you when needed.

Stop and Reflect To Figure Out Your Feelings

Have you ever had difficulty labeling or putting your feelings into words? I know that is something I struggle with on occasion, especially when it concerns something especially important to me. It's not an easy thing to do, but the good news is you can get better at it through practice. It's a process that is a lot like learning to ride a bike. You take a couple of hard knocks, tumbles, and scrapes to the knees, but once you master how to keep your balance, it becomes what you can do without even thinking about it.

Emotions serve as messengers, often nudging us to pay attention to something important within or around us. Think about them like the personal alert messages on your phone that buzz when you have a new incoming message. Every emotion has its purpose, and no feeling is "good" or "bad." Your body is experiencing a massive amount of internal growth and changes, which also means that your brain and body aren't always on the same page, and this can result in you feeling out of sorts. Learning to identify your feelings can actually help you get better and better at managing your responses and understanding your body. Imagine the positive things that can happen if you can learn to do all these things.

So, let's begin with exploring some of the more common emotions that you may be feeling on a daily basis and see if we can figure out what they are trying to tell us by using something I call the **Stop and Reflect Method:**

ANGER

Have you ever felt super annoyed, to the point of getting angry, and didn't know why? The next time that you find yourself feeling angry, stop and reflect:

- Why am I upset?
- Did someone cross a line?
- Is there something that I need to defend?
- Does something feel unfair or unjust?

AGGRESSION

This is when you're in "protect mode," like your inner guard dog barking when it senses danger. If you're feeling this bubbling up inside of you, take a deep breath and follow it with a moment of stop and reflect:

- Why am I feeling so on edge?
- Do I feel like someone's out to hurt me somehow?
- Can I rethink the situation and change how I feel about it?
- Will some physical activity help me feel better?

DISCOMFORT

You know that weird feeling when something's off? Discomfort usually points to something that is taking you out of your comfort zone in one way or another. You can dive into that by stopping and reflecting on it a bit more:

- Why am I feeling this way? Is something bugging me?

- Did something happen that I'm not okay with?

- What is it that feels out of place?

- What doesn't sit right with me?

FEAR

Everyone gets scared, but that doesn't make it easier to deal with. Distinguishing between actual threats vs. perceived threats can help determine how to best cope with this emotion. When you're feeling fear, try digging into it a bit by stopping and reflecting:

- Why am I freaked out? Is it a real danger, or is this worry about getting my feelings hurt?

- Is this fear about something that is really happening, or is this just a bad vibe?

- If I'm honest with myself, what am I really afraid of?

JEALOUSY

Ever see something that belongs to someone else and think, "I wish I had what they have"? If you have, you're not a bad person; you're completely normal. Still, it isn't necessarily a "feel-good" emotion, is it? Jealousy can be a clue to you about something your heart desires. If you're finding yourself feeling jealous, here are some things to stop and reflect on:

- What am I worried about missing out on?
- What do I secretly want?
- What am I afraid of losing?
- What is it that I would like also to have? Is this something that I can work on?

JOY

Remembering the good stuff helps you find more of it in the future. Joy is a beautiful emotion that needs celebration! When you notice what makes you happy, it helps you do more of that and spend time with the people who lift you up. Stop and reflect to store up those good memories:

- Why am I so happy right now?
- What or who lit up my day?
- What do I most want to remember about this moment?

Okay, I think you've got the point here. "Stop and Reflect" is the way to go when you are looking to dig a little deeper into what you are feeling and why. So the next time you're caught in a whirl of feelings, take a second to decode what might be going on for you and if there's something you can do to change the situation or how you feel about it.

Dealing With Disappointment

We don't get to choose what events life throws along our way, and most of those events come in completely unannounced and catch us off guard. Some people choose defeat in these kinds of situations, while others choose to rise again; they decide and declare for themselves that this disappointment is not a disadvantage. In other words, it's not the challenge or emotion that defines us but how we respond to it that does.

I used to be somewhat of a perfectionist; I set really high standards for myself, and it was always "go for gold" because if that's not what you're striving toward, what are you even doing? That way of thinking was helpful in some situations, but mostly, it set me up for major disappointment if things did not turn out the way that I expected. I was so hard on myself and didn't speak to myself very kindly when those outcomes were not as I hoped.

I still like to challenge myself, but now, I do it with a measure of self-compassion. I understand that I am an imperfect human being living a real life, which means that things will not always work out in the way I want them to. And I don't know about you, but it really used to irk me when someone would say, "Well, look on the bright side..." when I really just wanted to sit around and sulk. It can be very unpleasant to deal with things not working out, but it is a part of life.

Looking for the brighter side of things is sometimes easier said than done, but the one thing we can always fall back on is this: **the power of choice**. When disappointment comes knocking on your door, you may give in to that urge to stop moving forward because you may not feel like you have much of a choice.

And yet, it is during those times when it is most helpful to harness the power of choice that we all have but don't always know how to put into practice. This means that when you experience disappointment, you have options, or choices, as to how to respond to it. Granted, some disappointments are more difficult to cope with than others, but the power of choice is always within you. I'm going to give you a real-life example of what this looks like, and as you read this next teen's experience with disappointment, think about your own experience and feelings about disappointment and see if his experience feels familiar to you.

Jacob's Diamond Dreams

I would like to introduce you to another teenage acquaintance of mine- we'll call him Jacob. Jacob is a tall, sun-kissed 15-year-old sophomore who is really into baseball and REALLY wants to be on his high school's baseball team. He plays other sports, too, but the one that he's really passionate about is baseball.

This past summer, Jacob practiced his swing and pitch for two to three hours every single day. Every morning, the metallic clink of the bat meeting the ball or the swooshing sound of the ball slicing through the air was a testament to his family, friends, and neighbors of how dedicated he was to getting on the team. As summer faded and fall came in with a new year and a new opportunity for team tryouts, Jacob approached the day with a mix of nerves, excitement, and confidence because he had prepared so much.

The day after tryouts, Jacob stood amidst a crowd of other anxious hopefuls as they waited for the coach to post the names on the bulletin board. When the list went up, one by one, the players stepped forward, searching for their names to confirm that they had made it on the team. When it was Jacob's turn to read the list, his eyes darted across the sheet – once, twice, and then a crushing third time. Oh, no... his name wasn't there!

The coach was still nearby and, sensing his disappointment, approached him and said, "Hey Jacob, I'm glad that you tried out this year because I was able to see that you've got some real potential," he began, clapping a hand on Jacob's shoulder, "you're very close, but you're not quite there yet. I hope to see you at tryouts next year."

The world around Jacob became a blur, each word from the coach echoing painfully in his ears. Now what? It's all that he had wanted and prepared for. Jacob was crushed with disappointment.

The Power of Choice

Outcome #1:
Going Down The Rabbit Hole of Disappointment

The days that followed took on a grey hue for Jacob. The bat and ball, once his favorite things to play with, lay untouched in the corner of his room. He almost couldn't bear seeing them because they were constant reminders of his failure. Instead of continuing to practice his swing and pitches out on the field, Jacob chose the confinement of his room, the walls of which seemed to close in with each passing day.

Friends invited him to hang out, but he declined. The embarrassment, the thought of facing sympathetic glances or hushed whispers, was too much for him to endure. *"Everybody must be talking about what a failure I am!"* was the thought that went through his mind every single day. The sparkle in his eye dulled, replaced by a persistent cloud of disappointment that he did not feel strong enough to do anything about. As time passed, Jacob's friends continued to reach out, but with each refusal from Jacob, the invitations to hang out became fewer and fewer.

Every day, Jacob thought about what the coach said to him but only focused on the part where he stated, "... you're not quite there yet..." and did not want to consider the rest. Jacob began to struggle with his self-esteem and decided that he would probably fail at any other sports, so what's the point in trying anyway?

Outcome # 2:
Using Disappointment To Fuel His Motivation

The initial sting of disappointment was raw and painful, and Jacob allowed himself to wallow a bit in self-pity. Feeling sad and disappointed was normal, especially given all of the practice and hope that he had built up in his head about making it on the team. However, Jacob decided that he would not let what happened to him define him.

After allowing himself a couple of days to grieve, he picked up his bat, feeling its familiar weight in his hands, and thought to himself, "Okay, so he said I have potential, but what does that mean, exactly?" Instead of trying to figure it out himself, Jacob decided to go straight to the source and reached out to the coach: "What can I improve on? I really want to make it on the team next year, so if you can give me some help with that, I would really appreciate it."

With this new feedback in hand, Jacob was able to focus on improving his swing and implemented some of the tips that the coach had given him. He was super psyched and trained harder than ever! Jacob also decided that training alone or with a friend was not enough for what he wanted, so he joined a local league, ensuring he was always playing and improving. His friends noticed what a great attitude he had taken and admired how he took that "no" and made it a "yes!" for himself. Jacob's determination to turn a setback into a setup for a comeback was inspiring. By the following year, not only did he make the school team, he was also extremely well-liked for his ability to stay motivated in the face of the team's losses.

So, what's the moral of Jacob's story? The two outcomes show the power of choice and how one boy's reaction to disappointment quite literally changed the trajectory of his journey, and the same can happen for you. That being said, disappointments DO often come with feelings of sadness, annoyance, or even anger, so allow yourself to feel your feelings, but remembering that you always have a choice helps keep you feeling empowered to know that just because something didn't work out doesn't mean you're stuck.

Six Tips for Dealing With Disappointment

Jacob's story was short and told in a simple manner, but we all know that, in reality, dealing with disappointment is not always as easy as that. If you're still unsure what to do or how to react when things don't quite go your way, don't worry, I'm here to help. By putting the tips below into practice, you will grow closer and closer to being able to bounce back quickly and turn those disappointments into something quite amazing! That's what we call being resilient.

Tip #1:

Acknowledge that you have just been disappointed, and give yourself time to feel your feelings. Feelings that come after a disappointment don't just magically go away. We need to acknowledge that they exist and that we may be behaving a certain way due to how we feel. You can't change what you don't acknowledge, so lean into what you're feeling, and take it from there.

Tip #2:

Confide in someone and let it out. I know that this is a hard one, especially for boys and young men, who are so often taught by society that expressing feelings of sadness or disappointment is a sign of weakness. But if you want to become emotionally healthier and stronger, one way of doing that is by talking about your disappointment and the feelings that come with it. Talk to a friend, a family member, a teacher, or anyone you feel safe around. Verbalizing the disappointment will help you be more in control of your emotions and allow whatever it is that you are feeling to pass much faster than if you keep it in and just hope it goes away on its own.

Tip #3:

Reflect on the situation. It's so easy to catastrophize things and make them much bigger than they actually are. For example, thinking that your whole life is practically over because you didn't get the desired grade on that test that you spent days studying for or didn't make it on the team of your choice. Taking time to reflect on and work through that disappointment can help bring more clarity to the situation and decide if there is something different that you can do the next time around.

Tip #4:

Let go of the "What if." What if I had studied for three extra hours or hadn't spent those extra hours with my friends? What if I had eaten a better breakfast? What if I had worn my lucky shirt? What if... what if... what if...

The reality is that you will never know the answer to the "What if" question, and dwelling too much and too long on it can turn into anxiety, bitterness, and negative self-talk. If you find yourself starting to go down the "What if..." road, try to remind yourself that it is, quite literally, an unanswerable question, and see if you can refocus on questions that may be more helpful to finding a solution to your situation.

Tip #5:

Be kind to yourself. You are allowed to mess up and make mistakes. You owe it to yourself to let that kind heart be kind to yourself. With kindness, you'll always come out at the other end feeling better than before. Choosing kindness means choosing positive self-talk and choosing to champion and root for yourself in the now. A few things I like to tell myself when things don't quite go my way are:

- Regardless of the outcome, I am so proud of myself for giving it my all.

- I did the best I could with what I had, and now I have more information to learn from for the next time.

- Dealing with this disappointment is hard; it's okay to feel this way about this situation. All I need is time, and I know I will be okay.

- Disappointment is something that comes and goes. I'm choosing to not let it linger forever.

- It's okay to feel disappointed about how things turned out.

Tip #6:

Adjust your expectations. It is important to recognize that when we set goals for ourselves, we might also be met with obstacles along the way. So, in such situations, it certainly helps to measure your expectations and consider that potential obstacles do exist. Should you face disappointment along the way, having accepted that this is part of the journey will help reduce the sting that often accompanies disappointment.

Talking to Moms, Dads or Guardians About Your Emotions

I know what some of you must be thinking as you read that heading: *Why would I want to talk to them about how I feel?*

While parents/guardians have a lot of wisdom to add to your life, you don't always want it, do you? Yeah, I know; They offer you advice when you haven't asked for it, they try to fix things for you when you want to be the one to figure things out, and they don't always know how to just "be there" for you without intervening.

Although they might not say it out loud and want to understand how to be there for you, becoming a teen is as new and different of an experience for you as it is for them. They don't always know how to best support you during this stage of your life, so you'll do yourself a huge favor if you teach them how to by clueing them in as to how they can be helpful.

Parents/guardians often jump into "fix it" mode when they feel or see that something is wrong. It makes sense that they would do that because not only do they want to protect you, but they may also still see you as that cute 6-year-old who needed help learning to tie their laces or whose hand they needed to hold while crossing the street. It's hard to acknowledge that you're growing up and don't need them in the same ways you needed them before, so unless they get some idea from you about how you've now changed, they will probably continue to do the same things over and over.

"The conversation" doesn't have to be a big to-do, and the first thing I would tell you is to be in the right frame of mind. In other words, if you are upset or angry, then this is probably not the right time to have that talk with them, or with anyone for that matter. However, if you're in a good place, maybe having breakfast together or even waiting until the next time that they ask you, "So, what's going on?" you may want to take that opportunity to say something like:

"Well, I have something going on in my friend group, and I want to tell you about it, but I just need you to listen and not give me advice. Is that okay with you?"

Alternatively, if you do want their input, you might say something like this:

"Okay, so there's a bunch of drama going on with my friends, and I keep getting caught in the middle. I want your opinion on this, but I don't want you to get upset if I don't handle it how you think I should. Are you okay with that?"

If your parent/guardian continuously pries or insists that you tell them what is happening, it can often make you feel more upset and closed off. I know that you aren't doing this to intentionally hurt them or because you don't like them. More than likely, it is because you either aren't ready to talk about your feelings or don't even know how you feel, so how do you put that into words? Parents/ guardians may have different reasons for continuing to pry or insist you talk to them. Some may be confused by the change in the relationship. Others may be genuinely concerned that you are in trouble and don't have anyone else to turn to other than the source: You!

Once again, timing matters, and having that talk under the right circumstances will make all the difference. When you have found the right time to drop this knowledge on them, you might say something like this:

"Mom, I know that you worry when you see me upset and staying in my room, and sometimes, I do that because I just need the space to calm myself down. But other times, I go to my room because you keep asking me what's wrong, and I don't really want to talk about it, or I just don't know how to explain what's going on.

I usually come out when I'm feeling better, and if I want to talk about it, I'll let you know. I just need to know that you're not going to be upset at me for not wanting to talk about it, but I do know you're always there for me if I need you."

Or this:

"I'm feeling really bad about what happened, and I really just want you to listen and be there for me, please."

Or this:

"Honestly, I just need a hug right now."

In one way or another, everyone wants to be seen and have their feelings acknowledged, so learning how to communicate in a way that will help you get what you need is one of the most important life skills to hone in on, especially on your home turf. But parents/guardians are imperfect humans, so yes, they will definitely mess up sometimes and anger or upset you. Therefore, I want to share some thoughts and advice which I hope will help you to get on a successful path to better communication with them:

They are there to support you. Being "supported" won't always look like what we want it to look like. Sometimes, it looks like a hug and a comforting kiss on the forehead. Other times, it can look like being brought your favorite treats when you're having a hard time. On some other occasions, it can sound like a "no," even when you desperately want to hear a "yes."

Try to understand what you're feeling before heading into the conversation. Understanding your feelings will also help them understand what you're feeling, which could lead to a more productive conversation between you. For example, if you're nervous, you can start the conversation by saying something like this: *"I feel a bit nervous and somewhat awkward about what I am about to say, but I would really like to get your advice about this issue I'm dealing with."*

Start by making casual conversation first. Allow yourself to ease into the conversation by starting out with small talk. What do you normally talk about at the breakfast table, having dinner, or when you've just returned from school? Talk first about how your day was or about something interesting or funny that happened throughout the day. Small talk isn't always all that small, and it can help keep the lines of communication open between you and your parents.

Be observant and pick the best time to talk to your parents or the parental figure. Suppose, for example, that they are busy with something, i.e., working or talking on the phone, and you choose this time to ask them about something important. Chances are that you won't get their attention and may even get shooed away, none of which feels good. The better option might be to approach them and ask, *"Do you have a couple of minutes to talk?"* If they can chat, pull them to a quiet place with minimal distractions and do your thing. In summary, it's best to approach them when they are not very busy and can pay attention to what you're saying.

Clarify how it is that you want them to help. What would you like them to do after you've poured your heart out to them? Is there some advice that you would like them to give you, or do you just want them to listen? Do you just need a hug, their presence, and that acknowledgment that they will always be there for you and show up when you need them? Specify what it is that you want from them. So many of us fall short in the sense that we make the assumption that people already know what we want or need. People aren't psychic, and we shouldn't expect them to be either.

Seeking Out Other Support

Remember that situation that I told you about, the one where my best friend accused me of liking her boyfriend and then iced me out? When things got really emotionally tough, I reached out to someone I trusted - one of my aunties. She was my listener, my cheerleader, my shoulder to lean on. She reminded me I wasn't alone, even when I felt like I was. In her own way, she also let me know that I was totally normal for feeling this way, even when I felt utterly abnormal and didn't like myself very much. She also helped me to see the unfairness of it all and didn't shame me for still wanting to be friends with her. I didn't always share what I was going through, but it sure felt great to feel seen, heard and understood.

You don't need a massive amount of friends to get the support that you need, but is it sometimes hard to reach out? Heck yeah! Whether you are an extrovert who has no problem chatting it up with anyone or are shy and prefer to keep to yourself, asking for help or support can feel daunting. In some families, asking for help is frowned upon or considered a sign of weakness. I'm here to tell you that it is absolutely, 100%, unequivocally NOT a sign of weakness. As a matter of fact, asking for help is a sign of strength!

It takes courage, self-awareness, humility, and bravery to admit that you need help to figure some things out. We can all learn from someone else, and this can be especially helpful when that "someone else" can give us a different perspective or offer a solution that we may not have considered.

If you are struggling with a problem and can't figure it out or simply need someone to hear you out, consider reaching out to someone you trust. Take a moment to think about who you have in your life that you feel comfortable talking to. Perhaps it is your mom, dad, cousin, or another family member. Maybe there is a teacher, coach or counselor who you feel would be a good listener.

Always remind yourself that you do not have to face your problems alone. As you can see from that list, there are probably more people than you think who are available and willing to be there for you.

You are important and deserve to be heard, so give someone a chance to be there for you if you need a little help.

Think About It...

Phew, this has been a long, hopefully, insightful and eye-opening chapter. It's okay if you need a bit of a breather to process all that information. Once you've allowed the information to settle into your heart and brain, take a moment to stop and reflect on everything you've learned in this chapter. Here are questions to guide your thoughts.

1. What are two things you can do right now to get better at expressing your emotions?

2. Can you think of one thing that would change for the better if you get better at expressing your emotions?

3. Think about a conversation you would like to have with your parents/ guardians but haven't brought yourself to do it. What do you want to talk with them about most? What talking points do you want to bring up and not forget?

MY THOUGHTS

CHAPTER 4

Self-Image Matters

W ould you believe me if I told you that even the most confident people deal with self-esteem issues? Whether we realize it or not, we constantly compare ourselves to others in person and online, rarely considering how edited or filtered their images might be. We think to ourselves: *Why can't I be as skinny? Why can't I be as curvy? Why can't I be as ripped? Why can't I be as tall? I wish I had that six-pack!* It's important to remember that the internet is a virtual reality, and not everything we see is the whole truth.

Self-image, or how we see ourselves, is important to talk about because it can influence our thoughts, emotions, behaviors, and interactions with others. How we perceive ourselves can affect our self-esteem, self-confidence, and overall well-being. When we have a positive self-image, it becomes much easier to be assertive, communicate well, and create healthy relationships. It can also help us feel more confident and capable in our abilities, which can, in turn, lead to better outcomes in different parts of our lives.

When we have a negative self-image, we may be more prone to social anxiety or feelings of inferiority, making it challenging to connect with others or form deep relationships. Not to mention, it can also leave us feeling insecure, self-doubting, anxious, or sad. We're all human and vulnerable to feelings of insecurity, and this is especially true when you are a teenager trying to figure out who you are or want to be while watching others who are "already there" looking as if they are living their best lives. Body image is a particularly difficult issue at any age or gender, so I thought it worthwhile to share Kayla's experience with self and body image struggles.

Kayla's Struggle With Herself

Meet Kayla, a 15-year-old girl who has been struggling with body image for some time now. Kayla is friendly, funny, and well-liked by her peers. For as long as she can remember, she has been involved in various activities like dance, soccer, and softball. She has always been very active and has a naturally athletic build. But Kayla has a secret—despite being well-liked and included in everything by her friends, Kayla constantly compares herself to the other girls in her class and always comes to the same conclusion: They are all so much smarter, funnier, and, above all else, skinnier. Kayla was always worried about what other people would think or say about her. As you can imagine, living in this constant state of negative self-talk started to affect her mental state.

Kayla's struggle with her self-image is based on the things that she feels insecure about and not necessarily on *reality*. If Kayla were to take a step back and consider all of the things she was insecure about, she might find that she was being very hard on herself. The truth was that not all the other girls were as bright, as funny, or skinnier than her. Sure, her body type is not the same as her friend's, Emily, who is naturally tall and lanky, but trying to achieve a body type that is not genetically possible is a pretty impossible feat, wouldn't you say?

What might be more helpful to Kayla is if she were to look at her body and take notice of the things that she likes about it: her strong legs, her speed and agility, and how her favorite pair of jeans fit her body type so well.

With regards to "everyone else" being funnier and smarter, we have to once again ask Kayla to consider: is that really true? Yes, *__some__* others will be funnier and smarter, but not "everyone." Most importantly, Kayla is not considering what her friends like most about her: Her kindness and ability to cheer them up when they most need it. **The things that she is most loved for don't require that she be the funniest, smartest, or skinniest.** We've all been in Kayla's shoes. We've all thought to ourselves, *"I am not good enough,"* or *"I'll never measure up to those other people."* When we do this, we dim our own light and prevent that fierce inner magic from shining through us. Despite all that stuff that might be swirling around in your head, here is something that I want you to know:

You are worthy of all things good.

You deserve to live a life that aligns with your own version of joy.

You are remarkable, talented, and unique, and the world needs that magic of yours that you have to offer.

Cultivating a positive self-image and self-acceptance is essential for your mental and emotional health. And the reality is that those negative self-thoughts are rarely based on facts; instead, they are based on fears. The following sections will offer you some ways to start on the road to creating a positive self-image.

Dealing With Self-Esteem Issues

Self-acceptance can definitely be challenging. Our social media timelines are flooded with images of people with fantastic fashion sense and tanned bodies that look like they were sculpted by a 3D printer. It seems natural that we would compare ourselves to what we see because if they can look like that, then so can we, correct? Surely, we must then be lacking in something, right? But no, that's not necessarily the case, and it's time to put an end to that never-ending cycle of comparison. I want this win for you!

Wear clothes that make you feel good about yourself.

How do you feel about the clothes you wear? I'm not talking about labels or influencer-level stuff. I'm talking about how you actually feel in the clothes you are wearing on a daily basis. Your clothes are an extension of your personality and self-image, so by wearing clothes that you are comfortable with, you're essentially saying, *"This is me, and I love myself for being as I am. I will not change or be ashamed of who I am because society says I don't fit into its mold of what it means to feel good."*

If you are constantly dressing in clothes that make you feel self-conscious and insecure or don't reflect who you are, you will find it difficult to feel good walking around in them. So, my first suggestion would be to start by wearing clothes that make you feel good about yourself and how you want to show up in the world. Whether it is a hoodie, a dress, or a pair of goth boots, be who you are and let the world know that you're comfortable in your skin (even if you're still working on that!).

Surround yourself with people who don't body shame.

These kinds of friends encourage and root for body acceptance and body positivity. Negative attitudes and behaviors are seriously contagious, so if you surround yourself with people who constantly criticize others or each other about body image, you're very likely to also start adopting those same habits. Gravitate towards those who make you feel emotionally lighter and happy to be around, and you'll also feel happier.

Do things that bring you joy.

When was the last time that you made yourself smile? I know that sounds silly, but humor me and take a moment and think about that question. If it's been a while, take some time out and treat yourself because you deserve it and just because you can. It can be the simplest of things, like going to a park and going right for the swings, just like you did when you were a little kid. Doing things that bring you joy and lightness can take the focus away from your body and make you look toward those other things that matter, such as meaningful friendships, purpose, and self-care.

Find the one thing you like about yourself that doesn't relate to your body.

Perhaps you're a gifted singer, a creative writer, love to draw, or are known for making the most awesome bracelets, and all of your friends love wearing the ones you make for them. Liking yourself for all those things you have to offer and bringing them to the table makes body acceptance easier for us by making us realize that our bodies grant us the privilege to do all those things.

Be kind to other people.

I've talked a lot about how important it is to practice kindness with yourself, and now, I'll expand that to include other people. Kindness is powerful and also has a contagious nature about it. It touches the lives of those with whom we share it and our own lives. So, if you need help finding something you like about yourself, find something in other people you like. Compliment their eyes, their smiles, or their infectious personalities. In finding the good in others, we may find the good in ourselves.

How to Start Accepting Your Body

Here are a few things that I would say to every teen out there so that they can always remember that body changes are a normal part of life:

- A small body does not necessarily mean a healthier body; a bigger one does not necessarily mean an unhealthy one.

- Focus on feeding and fueling your body with foods that leave you feeling full and better, not full and sluggish.

- Our bodies are remarkable, capable of doing the most amazing things, regardless of size.

- Your body is carrying you through these multiple seasons of life; when you can, don't forget to be kind to that body of yours.

- It's okay if body acceptance does not necessarily mean body love. It's completely okay and normal if there are certain parts of your body that you are struggling to love right now. But just because you're finding it hard to love your body, it doesn't mean you have to constantly fight it.

- This relationship that you have with your body is the longest relationship you're going to ever have. Some days will be good, while some days are going to be harder than others. But regardless of what you're feeling, you still deserve to shower yourself with kindness and compassion.

- You don't have to be ashamed of gaining or losing weight. It says nothing about your worth or your value as a human.

- You have every right to stand up for yourself when someone comes up to you and criticizes how you look. Body acceptance is also about the boundaries we set to protect ourselves from people's unsolicited opinions.

- Be intentional about the types of messages that you absorb. In essence, be mindful of who you follow on social media. Be mindful of who you spend most of your time around because those things directly impact how we see ourselves. So, change your feed settings so that they hide all of those negative messages about fad diets and weight loss. And if someone you follow starts promoting diet culture messages you don't care for, don't be afraid to hit unfollow or block.

- Highlight and celebrate those things that you love about yourself. One of the best ways to do this is through journaling. You can call it your place of positive thinking, and each time a negative thought surfaces, you can counteract it with a positive one. We are much more prone to point out negative things; being intentional and making a list focusing on the positive things will incline you to think more positively about your body.

- Limit or stop comparing yourself to others. The beauty of being human is that we all come in different shapes and sizes. I mean, how boring the world would be if we all looked the same, don't you think? Comparing yourself to another person who is not meant to look like you only robs you of the joy and experience of appreciating yourself right now as you are.

Dealing with The Social Scene and Peer Pressure

We've talked a fair bit about social media and how deceptive it really is. And for good reason. Many people tend to look at other people's lives online, only to start thinking that there is something they're missing out on or something that is not going right for them in their lives.

The thing that we should all remember is that people only show you what they want you to see. They'll selectively filter everything else out and show you everything they think is perfect to show publicly. They'll want you to see their "perfect" beautiful house. Their fancy gadgets, all of their cool friends, and those great places they always hang out in, but what they most likely don't want you to know, or let's say what they won't let you see, is how lonely they feel. Or how those so-called friends of theirs aren't really good at all.

If we spend too much of our time trying to measure up with those people, we might end up with something called social perfectionism. When you're a social perfectionist, you have this deep-rooted fear that you aren't good enough or don't measure up, and you measure yourself according to how people see your social standing.

This brings to mind our friends and how much influence they tend to have over us. There's always that nagging fear that *"If I don't go along or do whatever they're doing, I will be left out and labeled the odd one out."* Sometimes, that's okay, but the truth is that we mostly want to fit in. The problem is that sometimes fitting in means doing things that you would never consider doing. Sometimes, these are things you come up with on your own, but most of the time, it is due to peer pressure.

Cliques vs. Friends

The first thing that I want to build on is the fact that there is a difference between cliques and friend groups.

Cliques are usually defined as an exclusive and specific group of people who hang out together. Cliques are typically closed to allowing new people "in" and are usually considered "judgy." People in cliques are generally controlled by the most influential person in the group. If someone from the clique develops outside friendships, they may face rejection and ejection from the group.

Friend groups are typically defined as groups of people who have similar likes, activities, or connections. They hang out together but are open to letting new people into the group. People in different friend groups socialize with others who may not be part of that same group, which is totally okay.

Whether you are part of one group or the other, you may still experience peer pressure. Peer pressure happens when you are pressured or strongly encouraged to act in ways that go against your values, beliefs, or even personality to fit in with the group. Many teens and adults fall prey to peer pressure because they want to feel they have friends who will have their backs.

The thing is that real friends do not use peer pressure to get you to do things that you are not comfortable with. Real friendships give you a sense of trust, enjoyment, and a feeling of safety and security. They have your back without you needing to compromise who you are for them to be there for you.

How Leah Got Her Cool Back

Let's walk a mile in the shoes of Leah, a vibrant 14-year-old taking her first steps into high school. In middle school, Leah was the sunshine on a cloudy day and had an infectious laugh. She had a close group of friends who became like family. Each friend held a unique bond with Leah, woven with threads of shared memories and inside jokes. When the weight of school's challenges bore down on her, it was to these friends that Leah turned, seeking solace in their comforting words and familiar smiles. They created a safe space, a cocoon where Leah could voice her fears and insecurities without judgment.

However, shifting to high school was like stepping into a different world. The corridors seemed to echo with uncertainty, the faces unfamiliar, and the routines felt completely alien to what Leah had been used to. Suddenly, Leah, who once seemed to dance through life, now felt like she was tiptoeing on eggshells. This unfamiliar territory brewed a bunch of new and uncomfortable feelings inside her: a dash of anxiety, a sprinkle of doubt, and a heavy dose of intimidation.

Have you ever felt like Leah, lost in a sea of new experiences and unsure how to cope? Guess what? You're not alone. Every change, particularly huge ones like starting high school, comes with challenges. For the first time in her life, Leah is experiencing feelings she can't even name: the yearning for old comforts of her middle school friends, the flutter of anticipation of making new ones, the tight knot of hesitation before trying something new. Recognizing these subtle feelings can be like solving a jigsaw puzzle; for Leah, every day might bring a new piece to fit in.

Leah could feel the weight of her worries as she thought about the daunting maze of high school corridors and the unfamiliar faces. She knew she couldn't let these fears dictate her new school experience, so she remembered some psychology techniques that her older cousin, Danielle, had once told her about. Leah decided to reach out to Danielle for help because the thought of going through high school feeling like this was just not an option!

First, Leah knew that she needed to change her thinking to start feeling better; this is where her cousin's help was a total homerun. Leah has given me permission to share a bit of her personal journal, so here is a peak for you and, quite literally, take a page out of her book:

A PAGE FROM LEAH'S JOURNAL

Sept. 9th

Ugh, today was a tough day to get through, but here I am again, confiding in you because this is actually helping. Thank goodness for Cousin Danielle and the guide that she gave me to help figure this all out! Okay, here we go:

The PROBLEM or situation I faced:

- The girls' volleyball team tryouts were today and I didn't know anyone there.

My THOUGHTS about the problem/situation:

- Everybody seemed to already know each other- I'll never fit in!

- No one is going to want me on their team.

My FEELINGS about the problem/situation:

- I feel so stupid for being here.

How REALISTIC are my THOUGHTS?

- If I think about it, not everyone really knew each other.

- One girl is in my history class and I know for sure that she moved here from another town, so she would not have known anyone either.

- Also, some of the girls smiled at me while they waited for their turn.

Are there OTHER WAYS of looking at this problem/situation?

- If I make it to the team, I will have a whole new set of friends with something in common.

- Maybe some of the girls are just friendly and didn't really know each other from before.

- In middle school, we had a few kids transfer to our school who made friends and fit in just fine.

- I've been able to make new friends in new situations before, like at the new day camp.

After thinking about this more, how am I FEELING NOW?

- It's normal for me to not know anyone at a brand new school and others are in the same situation, so it feels less scary.

- Feeling proud of myself for trying out—it wasn't stupid of me to try.

Is there anything that I CAN DO to help myself feel better?

- I can maybe sit down for lunch with that girl from history class. She seemed pretty nice and can probably use a new friend too.

As you learn and practice this new way of thinking, be patient and gracious with yourself. This process takes time; no one expects you to be comfortable with it from the start. So, keep going even if you don't find the right words you want to use. Learning is a process, so continue paying attention and noticing how you feel over time. You might surprise yourself at how much progress you're making!

Know Who You Are

The first step in choosing who to surround yourself with is knowing yourself and who you are. Take a moment to pay close attention to what you do and what matters to you most. Do you worry too much about what your friends think? Do you have to worry about this with your current friend group?

Next, think about the people from your past and present who have made you feel really great during and after you have spent time with them. Are they funny, silly, kind to each other? Do you feel safe speaking to them about stuff on your mind and vice versa? What are the things that you have in common, and what are the things that make each of you unique?

Surround yourself with people who are imperfectly perfect and who won't judge or make fun of you for being imperfectly perfect, either. Allow yourself to do things imperfectly. Allow yourself to fail and to be messy. The pictures you post don't have to be perfectly filtered or curated. When I think about this, I think about those social media influencers who give me a genuine and honest depiction of what it really looks like to live a day in their lives. Those influencers who show the good and imperfect aspects of their lives remind me that I am not alone in my struggles and that they are also people with flaws.

Try not to worry too much about saying the right things or acting perfectly when you're with your friends. I truly believe that if our friends care about us as much as they say they do—when you meet and find the right kinds of friends for you—they won't force you to be or turn you into something you aren't. They will accept you as you are, imperfections and all.

Do things because they mean something to you. Don't do things because you want to impress other people. Do them because they make you happy. I know this young girl who is in her early teens. She's a gifted writer who uses her favorite social media apps to share and showcase her work with her followers. She opened up once about how hard it was for her to continue sharing her work because it didn't get as many likes or views as the other creators on the platform. Still, when she started focusing on the joy that writing gave her, she began to find more fun in the process, which made it more fulfilling. She knew and understood that even though she wasn't reaching millions of people, she was still reaching a few, which was more than enough.

Tips For Managing Peer Pressure

Always think about the consequences of your actions. Here's a situation for you: Your friends want you to lie to your parents and tell them that you are going for a sleepover, but what they plan on doing is going to a party. What are the potential dangers of going to that party? What if you were to get into an accident, and as scary as it is to talk about, what if one of you were to get drugged by one of the older kids at the party? Before succumbing to that peer pressure, it's important to consider that your actions bear consequences, and those may affect you and the ones you love as well.

Delay tactics are quite a handy trick as well.

My all-time favorites are:

- "Let me get back to you."
- "I need to see if I will have time."
- "I have to ask my parents."

Try as much as possible to stay away from that peer pressure in the first place. My grandma had one thing to say about trouble: *"You have to stay away from it altogether!"* Well, Grandma, that's sometimes much easier said than done. But time and experience have taught me that this can be done by surrounding yourself with friends who have values similar to yours. You don't have to be a part of the "cool" group of kids if their actions don't align with how your parents/guardians raised you. The right kinds of people bring out the best in you. They enable and allow our lights to shine a little brighter, so think about your friends and how you feel around them. Do they make you feel crappy about how you are choosing to live your life, or are they, simply put, your biggest champions and advocates? Being aware of how you feel will absolutely help guide your friendship choices.

Find someone supportive. Those teenage years can be a pretty lonely place to be in, and that's valid because you are still learning how to figure things out for yourself. Worse, you are still learning to figure out yourself. Having someone to talk to and to share your frustrations with can help you find that reassurance that you are not alone in your struggles.

It's Okay to Ask For Help

Doing things alone without anyone else's help is pretty cool and badass. But you know what is even more cool and more badass? Acknowledging that you need help sometimes. **I am an adult, and I still have many days where I need to step back and admit that I can't do it all alone.** What about you? What do you do when you're struggling? Do you simply force yourself to get your act together, or do you offer yourself grace and compassion and relieve yourself from the pressure of carrying that burden?

Asking for help is a sign of maturity. It shows that you are aware of your strengths and weaknesses and are willing and open to letting people help fill the gaps in the areas where you fall short.

How do you ask for help when asking for help seems like an impossible thing to do? The following tips are relevant to any situation—a friendship-related issue, an issue regarding mental health, or a general question about adulting and growing up. I've got you covered.

- **Start with an adult whom you trust.** By trusted adult, I don't mean a parent or family member per se; you could approach a coach or a teacher. I still remember my relationship with my high school English teacher—she was a blessing in disguise, and quite frankly, I am so glad that I had her to turn to in times of uncertainty. I'm grateful for the wisdom and the encouragement she shared when I needed it most. If having a face-to-face conversation with them seems too daunting, consider sending an email or text message. Either way, they will be grateful that you reached out to them.

- **Use a teenage support group.** Group settings are particularly helpful in making us feel less lonely. The best part about a teenage support group is that you will encounter and chat with other teens facing similar challenges.

- **Practice, practice, practice.** As much as you ask for help with the big things, ask for help with the little things as well—it will make it much easier for you to practice asking for help in the first place.

If you caught a bad cold, you wouldn't shame yourself for needing to go to the doctor. So, don't feel ashamed or embarrassed about needing to talk to someone about life, other issues, and obstacles. You are human, and humans weren't made to exist perfectly. The messiness makes things all the more exciting.

Think About It...

I hope this was an especially helpful chapter for you. If you take away anything from it, I hope you discover what a remarkable human being you are and that the words shared shine a light on your remarkable qualities. And finally, I hope that you never forget that you are allowed to be loud and unapologetic about your dreams.

There is enough room for you on this place called Earth to show up and shine as the very best version of you. Before we move on to our next chapter, let's pause and think about everything covered in this chapter. Use these questions to guide your thoughts:

1. Are you too hard on yourself? If so, what is one way you can be kinder to yourself?

2. Are you worried about what your friends think of you? Are your friends and their values in line with who you are?

3. Do you feel your friends think poorly of you for any reason? Whatever that one thing is, think of it carefully. Is this worry based on reality or just your perception?

MY THOUGHTS

CHAPTER 5

Chill Skills For Managing Your Anger

A s we wrap up our discussions around the importance of being able to express your emotions, I couldn't end this section without chatting with you about something we all experience—anger. Everyone has emotions, and every emotion has a place in our lives. You've heard me say this before: Feelings aren't inherently good or bad—they're just signals telling us how we interpret the world around us.

But what about anger? Well, anger is just one of those many emotions, but it's gotten a bad rap. Anger can feel gigantic, like a roaring, fiery dragon, or tiny, like a little lizard. That's all normal because you're a teenager (and human). During these years, your brain grows and changes super quickly. This means you feel all emotions, including anger, more intensely. It doesn't mean you're out of control; it's just your brain's way of figuring things out.

Anger is as normal as feeling happy or sad, and it's a sign from your body telling you something isn't quite right. It's normal and natural and not something to be ashamed of.

Still, it can be a pretty difficult emotion for you or others around you to cope with.

The real trick is learning how to tame that angry dragon. To do this, you need to understand why you're angry, spot the things that make you feel this way, and learn some cool tricks to calm down because when anger starts ruling our lives, well, that's when we need to pull out our chill skills. The following list comes from one of my favorite resources for teen anger management skills: Chills Skills In A Jar (Free Spirit Publishing, 2021).

Ten Skills To Help You Chill...

1. Understand the 'Why' Behind Your Anger

Often, anger acts like a mask for deeper, more vulnerable feelings. Next time you're angry, take a moment to ask yourself: "What's really going on here?" Are you feeling hurt? Disappointed? Scared? Once you uncover the real emotion behind your anger, it will be easier to understand what you're actually upset about.

2. Recognize Your Triggers

Certain situations or people may push your buttons. It could be a specific situation, actions, or words from someone else. When you can identify your triggers, you can be better prepared to look out for them and be in a much better position to manage your reactions when they arise.

3. Stop and Think

Before reacting in anger, stop and think about your response. Tell yourself, "I can keep myself calm, even if I'm angry." Then, think and ask yourself: "Will yelling or lashing out help this situation? Is there a better way to express my feelings?"

4. Talk It Out

This may sound funny, but sometimes, role-playing what you want to say to someone you are upset with is super helpful! You can do this by asking a friend to play the person you are upset with and practice what you want to say. When you speak to the person you are having a problem with, tell them about your feelings calmly and respectfully. Use "I" statements to express your feelings, such as "I feel upset when...". Remember that you are more likely to be heard when speaking calmly than if you are yelling.

5. Practice Listening

Sometimes, anger arises from misunderstandings. Make sure you're really listening to what the other person is saying before you respond. If you want to ensure that you're hearing what the other person is saying correctly, practice "reflective listening," which means repeating back to the person what you heard them say to ensure that you heard it right.

6. Compromise

Not every disagreement has to be a win-or-lose situation. Still, sometimes, people are only willing to listen if they are getting what they want. A compromise involves both parties being open to looking for a middle ground that respects both your feelings and the other person's. This may mean not fully getting what you want, but there is a "win" for you in there somewhere.

7. Apologizing for Mistakes

Everyone messes up sometimes, and it can be hard to admit we're wrong. If you've done something wrong, a sincere apology can go a long way to mend the relationship. Another plus is that you will feel good about yourself for being brave enough to own up to your mistakes.

8. Practice Self-Compassion

You're going to have bad days. You're going to get angry and lose your cool sometimes. And that's okay. Practice self-compassion by reminding yourself that it's okay to be imperfect and it's okay to make mistakes. What's important is to learn from these experiences and keep trying to improve. Treat yourself with the same kindness you'd give a struggling friend when you slip up.

9. Finding a Calm Place

Find a peaceful spot where you can go to relax and let go of your anger. This could be a cozy corner in your room, a quiet spot in the park, or even a calming mental image. If you can't physically go anywhere, use the power of creativity that lives in that beautiful brain of yours. Imagine yourself in that calm place and allow the feelings of calmness to send soothing waves through your body.

10. Get Away

If a situation is escalating and you can't seem to cool down, or if things are getting out of hand with someone else, it's okay to walk away for a bit (as long as it's safe to do so). Give yourself some time to calm down before you try to tackle the issue again, or use the time to speak with someone who is supportive.

Remember, managing anger isn't about never getting angry—it's about experiencing and handling anger in a more healthy manner. So, take these tips, put them in your "chill skill" jar, and use them next time you need help keeping cool.

You've got this!

Think About It...

1. Are there skills from this list that you already use and find helpful? If so, under what circumstances or situations?

2. Can you think of a situation(s) where you might implement one of these skills? If so, what is the situation, and how do you think this new skill could help you?

MY THOUGHTS

CHAPTER 6

Critical Thinking Skills

What Critical Thinking Is And How It Can Help Teens

Imagine being a detective, piecing together a puzzle, discerning the connections to crack a case. Now imagine that just like that detective, you're skilled at sifting through bad data or wrong information and drawing the best conclusions from the facts you gather. And the more you practice, the more you evolve into a master of logical reasoning. Not bad, right? But why would you care about being able to decipher through information and draw the best conclusions? And more importantly, how does this matter in your daily life?

Let's start with tech talk. You're growing up in a digital age that is mind-blowing: viral memes, jaw-dropping apps, and challenges that become available to you seconds after being posted. But, as you've probably noticed, there's a flip side to all this good tech fun. The internet can also be a source of fake avatars, images, and false impressions of reality. And all that can, unfortunately, mess with how you make decisions in different aspects of your life.

With your critical thinking skills on point, you won't just be guessing at what's real, fake, or just plain incorrect; you'll be dissecting information and piecing things together that will allow you to make much better decisions based on fact and logic. **And the biggest bonus: You'll have the confidence to back up your decisions and defend your choices.**

Whether you are an 8th grader choosing a high school or a high schooler just starting to consider your next steps, making decisions with such high stakes can leave you feeling overwhelmed, with no idea which way to go. But decision-making skills, or critical thinking skills, don't only matter with the big stuff. As a matter of fact, they're important to have in your everyday life, with the smaller, less critical yet important daily decisions.

Since most of you are likely in the process of making a bigger decision, like what high school or college to attend, I'll tell you about how one student learned to use his critical thinking skills to reduce his anxiety and feel confident about his final choice.

Kaleb's College Confusions

Kaleb is a 17-year-old high school senior who is both excited and intimidated at the thought of choosing a college. Kaleb has always been a "do first, think later" kind of person who tends to do things without thinking, which has resulted in him making decisions that he later regrets. For example, when Kaleb first started applying for summer jobs, he took the first job that offered an easy, quick solution to his needs (a little extra spending money was all he wanted, really). Unfortunately, it was too rash of a decision. It didn't take him long to realize that dog walking six neighborhood dogs three times per day, from Monday to Friday, took away all his freedom to enjoy the short summer break. Not to mention, that was a lot of poop to pick up!

As college applications become a reality, Kaleb wants to be much more intentional about the type of summer jobs that he applies for. His dad had always talked to him about "using your judgment to make good decisions," but truthfully, he never really understood what his dad meant by that and wasn't all that interested in asking either. "Critical thinking." That's what his father would sometimes call it. "Critical what?" Kaleb asked.

Kaleb had always felt his father was too serious about this stuff and needed to chill out a little. Did he sometimes react before thinking and get in trouble? *"Sure, but what's the big deal?"* he thought to himself. *I'll learn to 'critically think' when I'm older—that's when I'll need it."* However, Kaleb now found himself in his senior year of high school, feeling overwhelmed by the options of colleges to apply to. He desperately wants these decisions to be much easier than they seem to be.

Kaleb's dilemma is a perfect example of how you can use critical thinking skills to help you rule out all of the extra gunk that you don't need, clogging up your brain pipes. Let's take a look at how Kaleb started to use critical thinking to help him sort things out.

Step 1: Met with his school counselor

Kaleb made an appointment to meet with Ms. Riley, his school and college guidance counselor, and explained his overwhelm and frustrations. Ms. Riley was a pro at this and had seen students like Kaleb in her office many times before– *"Don't worry, Kaleb, I'm going to work with you and give you a step-by-step guide that you can apply whenever you need to think through any decision that you need to make, and we'll start with deciding what colleges you want to apply to."* Phewwww! Upon hearing that, Kaleb felt an immediate sense of relief and was now motivated to move on this.

Step 2: Learned the 4 key steps of critical thinking skills

Ms. Riley took out a one-page worksheet that had two columns. On the left column of the worksheet were the four steps, and the right column was blank next to each step. Kaleb knew they were getting to work right away, and now that he had a framework in front of him. He started to get psyched!

Step 3: Applied his new critical thinking skills

Here's how Kaleb used the worksheet to start working through his college decision problem:

Critical Thinking Skill	Considerations/ Solutions
Key Step 1 Identify the problem:	What colleges should I apply to that are best suited for my goals and preferences?
Key Step 2 Information gathering:	Kaleb and Ms. Riley concluded that these were the most important factors to consider: Admissions criteria, course offerings, campus vibe, location, tuition and internship opportunities. Now that this was clear, Kaleb narrowed down his search to colleges that would first fit the criteria that would be most important for him, which were admissions criteria, course offerings and location. He also took Ms. Riley's advice of creating a simple spreadsheet that would help him easily keep track of all of the information that he was about to gather and not become overwhelmed with information overload.
Key Step 3 Evaluating the evidence (information):	Kaleb needed to make sure that his information for these colleges were as up to date as possible and reliable. In order to do this, he worked with Ms. Riley to make sure that the sources of his information were reliable (and unbiased when necessary).
Key Step 4 Make the decision:	Armed with his amazing spreadsheet, fleshed out research and solid sources for the information that he gathered, Kaleb now felt very confident to dive right in. This method made it so much easier to compare the pros and cons of his top college choices.

As you can see from this example, Kaleb's new critical thinking skills made all the difference. By implementing them, he was able to:

Make an informed decision that wasn't swayed by shiny brochures or flashy websites. Instead, Kaleb was able to critically evaluate his options and make decisions based on insights, facts, and information that appealed to his personal goals and aspirations. As he combed through the information and used his critical thinking skills, Kaleb felt much more confident and less anxious about his final decisions.

Avoid decisions made on bias. Kaleb began to recognize what "bias" looked like and could steer clear of potential biases, like being tempted to apply to a college just because his friends were going there, which can be a pretty powerful bias with not-so-great long-term consequences!

Long-term benefits and outcomes were considered. Rather than just thinking about what freshman year would be like, critical thinking allowed Kaleb to consider how these different colleges would support his entire college journey and his potential career paths.

The magic of critical thinking is that you don't just learn how to fix a problem. You learn how to think through it, understand the root of the issue, and find a solution that works best, given all the facts and information. Critical thinking is a skill that you can apply to many of the big and small decisions that you will be making in your lifetime. Whether it's picking a college, deciding on a job, or even deciding on getting a pet, it's all about thinking clearly, weighing your options, and making choices you won't regret. And trust me, once you've got it down, you'll wonder how you ever managed without it!

Think About It...

You've gotten through another chapter—great job!! If you really take it to heart, then you will be equipped and prepared for success as you navigate your way through those future college or work interviews. Now, let's take a minute to reflect on what we've learned in this chapter. These questions will help you out.

1. Channel your inner detective: Always look beyond the obvious. Dive deep into the "whys" and "hows" of a situation.

2. Think about a past situation where critical thinking skills could have helped. How could things have turned out differently if they had utilized the strategies covered in this chapter?

3. Which of the critical thinking traits do you feel you're lacking in the most? What can you do to strengthen it?

MY THOUGHTS

CHAPTER 7

Personal and Practical Safety Skills

Personal Safety Skills

I love saying "yes" to people as much as I love a good steaming cup of hot cocoa in the wintertime. Saying "yes" makes me feel like I'm somehow being a good person or that people will like me more. So it's safe to say that I've said yes way too many times, and unfortunately, even to things I didn't want to say "yes" to. It's like a reflex. Sometimes, I say it without thinking; other times, I fear people won't like me if I say no. Rejection stinks, but you know what stinks even more? Feeling like you have not been true to yourself. But learning to say "no" is not just about being true to yourself. It can actually be a significant part of staying out of harm's way.

This chapter's first part focuses on helping you stop saying "yes" when you really want to say "no." We will look at different areas that require an extra check-in and some safety skills that will keep you ahead of potentially dangerous situations. Safety skills are essential because life can be pretty unpredictable, and things happen that land us in dangerous situations. It would be great to know that we will be quick and responsive in those moments, but it would be helpful to know what to look out for before we can do that. Let's start with discussing an area that cannot be stressed enough for growing teens like you: Personal safety.

Learning To Trust Your Gut

Growing up, we're often taught that being agreeable, nodding along, and saying "yes" is polite and friendly. And it makes sense. After all, who doesn't want to be liked and accepted? The allure of being part of the crowd can make it feel like saying "yes" is your golden ticket to being socially accepted or even loved.

But here's a little secret everyone needs to learn: there's immense power in the word "NO" and in certain situations, "NO" is enough and does not need further explanation. In specific circumstances, saying "NO" is not about being difficult or creating conflict, but rather, it is about learning to set boundaries that protect you by following that intuitive little voice inside you.

The intuitive voice I'm referring to is what people often call that "gut feeling." It's that feeling that nudges at you, making you question something or someone when something doesn't feel right. This unique feeling is also known as "intuition," and we are all born with this ability to sense when something is wrong. Intuition, or a "gut feeling," is one of the most potent tools Mother Nature has given you to protect yourself. Sometimes, it's the one voice in your head telling you to say "no," even if everyone around you is saying "yes."

The power of intuition is such a fascinating concept that it has been explored in several different scientific circles, like psychology and neuroscience. And while it is something that we can use to "check-in" with ourselves for just about anything, we will focus on using it for safety.

Our brains are constantly picking up cues from our environment and processing the information on a subconscious level. This means that although you may not be consciously aware of all the environmental cues your brain is picking up and storing up for later use, just like the processor in your desktop or laptop, it is working behind the scenes at all times. Examples of cues your brain subconsciously picks up include body language, sensing fear, and threat.

When faced with a situation where you need to "act" before thinking, your intuition can help you make on-the-spot decisions that protect you from real or perceived threats. An easy example we can all relate to is catching a glimpse of an object coming in our direction, which may hurt us if it hits us. In that moment, your intuition is one of the factors that help you make the quick decision to move away or block the object before it hits you. Intuition also relies on recognizing patterns and emotional signals. This is why your "gut feelings" may signal you to not do something or when there is something potentially dangerous that you may want to avoid.

Our intuition is not entirely infallible, which is why it should be combined with some good, old-fashioned, rational decision-making. But if you're ever in a situation where you don't have time to think, or if what you're seeing is not sitting well, trust your gut!

Practice How To Say "NO"

There are times when your gut feeling is simply whispering, *"I'm not sure about this... this feels wrong or inappropriate"* in your ear. There are other times when your gut is screaming, *"NO, don't do it- get away from this as soon as possible!"*

Rather than share any stories with you about why learning to become comfortable with listening to your gut and learning to say "NO" is important, I'll share a list of real-life situations that you will want to seriously consider saying "NO" to, along with some responses that you can use (or create your own), and action steps that you can follow up with:

Situation:

Someone you barely know is pressuring you to attend a private party where no one you know will be.

Your Response:

"Thanks for the invite, but I'm gonna sit this one out. I usually only go to parties where I know my friends will be. Besides, I'm pretty sure my parents have secretly installed some tracking thing on my phone and will hunt me down wherever I am."

Action Step:

Send a text about the invite to a close friend or family member, just so they know. It's always good to keep someone in the loop when you feel uneasy about a situation.

Situation:

A friend repeatedly pushes you to try something you're uncomfortable with, even after you've already declined.

Your Response:

"I'm not trying to be rude, but I already said I'm not into it. We can chill and do something else, but stop asking about that because I'm not down with it."

Action Step:

If they continue to push, consider leaving the situation. Let someone you trust know what's going on so they're aware in case you need support or a pick-up.

Situation:

Being around someone who constantly belittles or mocks others makes you question how they might talk about you behind your back.

Your Response:

"Why are you always ragging on people like that? I mean, it's making me wonder what you say when I'm not around."

Action Step:

If you're feeling targeted or uncomfortable, it's okay to distance yourself. Spend time with friends who lift you up and make you feel positive. If you need to process the situation, consider venting to a friend or trusted adult about how you're feeling.

Situation:

A new acquaintance seems to have an unusual amount of curiosity about your personal life, your family's finances, or other personal details.

Your Response:

"So, that information is kinda personal, and I'm not comfortable sharing that kind of stuff with anyone."

Action Step:

If they continue to be invasive, consider distancing yourself and talking to someone you trust about the situation. Keep an eye on how much personal information you share online or in group chats because they could also find out about you that way.

Saying "no" is a way in which we teach ourselves to value our time and space and keep healthy boundaries. But more importantly, it can be a word that keeps us personally safe and out of dangerous situations.

Toxic Relationships: Recognizing Warning Signs

Healthy relationships should feel balanced, fair, and supportive. But sometimes, without even realizing it, we might get involved with someone who brings out the worst in us or puts us in uncomfortable situations. In our quest to be liked or fit in, we sometimes overlook red flags or put ourselves in potentially dangerous situations.

Recognizing those red flags and mustering the courage to say "no" is not just about protecting your feelings. It is also about safeguarding your well-being. As a teen, you may be vulnerable to not recognizing those danger signs, and this has more to do with experience than anything else.

This is why learning to listen to and trust your gut is so important! In many situations, that intuition will warn you that something isn't right, even if you don't have much relationship experience. This is a topic that I feel deserves a whole book of its own, but for now, here are some signs that you may be encountering a toxic or troubling relationship:

They are always jealous of you spending time with anyone other than them

We all want to feel wanted because, let's be honest, feeling wanted also makes us feel special. These are completely normal things to feel and yearn for. It is also very normal to sometimes feel jealous because we all fear losing the things we cherish or secretly want something someone else has.

The problem occurs, however, when the person or people you are spending time with begin to express or act out feelings of jealousy that start making YOU feel like you are doing something wrong by spending time with other people. To complicate matters more, this behavior is often justified by the old *"I just like you so much that I want to spend all my time with you"* line. While that may be true, it is also a ***BIG RED FLAG***, and you should absolutely listen to your body when it is telling you that something doesn't feel right about it.

A healthy and secure relationship allows for the people in it to grow and experience new things, sometimes together and sometimes apart, without the need to feel bad about it if it is apart. Suppose, for example, you are spending time with someone who makes you feel uncomfortable, guilty, or ashamed about spending time with anyone else or doing anything that doesn't include them. **Without a doubt, this is a sign of an unhealthy relationship.** If you find that you are feeling this way, ask yourself the following questions:

- *Am I actually doing something wrong?*
- *Am I hurting anyone, breaking the rules or the law?*
- *Have I done anything that I deserve to be ashamed of?*
- *Is it fair for me to give up the things and people I like for this person to be happy?*

If your answer is "NO" to any of these questions, please consider if this is a relationship you want to continue being in and seek the support you need to get out of it.

They engage in behaviors that are meant to control you

This one is especially tricky because controlling behaviors aren't always obvious. I'll give you an example of a recent situation I was aware of. A parent started to notice a significant change in her 13-year-old daughter's behavior.

Her daughter had always been a very active and outgoing kid who kept close contact with a group of her middle school friends even after they went their separate ways. But something started to change. This sweet and outgoing girl, let's call her Dalia, began to spend a lot more time in her room, stopped speaking to her friends, and even decided to quit dance, which she had been studying since age 6 and absolutely loved. To top it off, she stopped chatting with her mother about her day, even though they had always been very close.

Dalia's mother became increasingly concerned and struggled about whether to check her phone. After all, they had a great relationship, and she did not want to violate her daughter's privacy, so she struggled with what to do. Ultimately, her concerns for her daughter's safety won out, and she looked through her child's phone. What she found left her confused, alarmed, and unsure of what to think.

Dalia had been communicating with someone for a couple of months now. At first, her mother did not know what to make of it because the person's name was in her contacts as "FINN143," and the communication with them looked like pure gibberish, which left her even more confused. She decided to take screenshots of a few conversations and see if she could make any sense of it.

I'll spare you the details of how she eventually figured it out, but what she discovered is worth sharing here! Dalia's mom was able to decipher that "FINN143" was a much older boy who had befriended Dalia. The texts between them had become increasingly inappropriate, with FINN143 pressuring her to send him photos of herself, and not the kind that she would readily share with the world!

Some of the coded text conversations were of FINN143 also telling Dalia that he loved her and that the only way she could prove her love for him was to be on call for him at all times. This meant that when he would text her the word "TIME," she would immediately be expected to text him back the time showing on her clock right at that moment! Dalia's mother also discovered that "FINN143" got her daughter to start doing this by saying it was a game they would play.

In addition, FINN143 was increasingly attempting to isolate Dalia from her friends. In one screenshot, he talked badly about them (even though he had never met them) and firmly declared they were "not her real friends." Dalia's mom knew this was the beginning of a dangerous and manipulative relationship that her young daughter was getting roped into. As she realized how much influence this person had on her daughter, she worried about approaching her without isolating her further.

As you can see from this example, controlling behaviors can start out looking very innocent—a sharing of a funny meme, a friend of a friend contacts you, or someone you don't know slowly slithers into your social media world, finds out about the things that matter to you through what you're posting and uses that information to befriend you. The reality is that you are growing up in a world different from your parents. You are exposed to more adult situations than your brain is developmentally ready for. It's got nothing to do with intelligence—it's simple biology. But if this is the world you are growing up in, I say we do what we can to help your brain deal as best as possible with all the extra stuff thrown at you this early on.

Other "Red Flag" Behaviors

Everyone has bad days and moments when controlling our emotions is just plain hard. However, if you are dealing with someone acting in ways that make it difficult to be around them or make you feel bad about yourself, physically or emotionally unsafe, or responsible for "calming them down," trust your instincts. I've listed some more behaviors to look out for below, and remember, if it doesn't feel right, then it probably isn't:

Acting out in a car

Fast, erratic driving or reckless driving that scares you and does not let you out of the car.

Unexpected or unwarranted explosive anger or rage while you're in the car.

Once in the car, you start getting bombarded with criticisms about how you look and act, or even things that have nothing to do with you, but you are criticized for them anyway.

Purposefully driving in ways that may cause you pain. For example, if you have an injury that you are nursing or are ill, and the person purposefully drives over potholes or rough terrain to make you feel discomfort or pain.

Road rage gets started by something that angers the driver, but then the anger gets targeted toward you.

You notice patterns of manipulative or deceitful behavior

This one's tricky because manipulation can be subtle like someone playing with your feelings or twisting words using an invisible wand. And guess what? Adults can also fall victim to manipulation and deception. One common manipulative behavior is frequently guilt-tripping another person. This means that you get blamed for something that, once again, has nothing to do with you, or they make you feel like you owe them. People in healthy relationships won't keep score or make you feel indebted to them, nor will they do things for you only to hold it over your head later.

Deceit, in particular, can show up as lying, hiding things, exaggerating, or leaving information out. One example of deceit teenagers often face can look like someone tricking you into drinking alcohol or using a substance that will get you high or "out of it" by disguising it as a game of Truth or Dare.

Another example of deceitful or manipulative behavior might be someone who constantly tells you that you can trust them with anything but then gets angry at what you tell them. You begin to feel obligated to tell them what they want while also fearing how they might react.

They are either causing drama, playing the victim or blaming you for their behavior

Suppose you hear things like, *"It's your fault that I get like this... I don't want to act like this, but you really push me to my limits."* This is a dangerously manipulative way of victim blaming and shaming, which is meant to make you feel responsible for how THEY act. If you're hearing anything that sounds even remotely close to that, it's time to carefully consider leaving this relationship in the safest way possible.

You are **NEVER** responsible for how anyone else acts or responds to any given situation, ever. You are only responsible for yourself and your own actions. If someone you are close to (or getting close to) gives you the sense that you are somehow responsible for their behavior, remember that **THEY are choosing to behave this way.**

As always, I encourage you to trust your gut, and if it does not feel right, or worse, you are feeling scared or hesitant, you are probably right. When something or someone feels too good to be true, take a step back and talk to someone you trust to help you evaluate the situation with a more objective view.

They dismiss your feelings, opinions, or boundaries

This can be another behavior that is difficult to catch because often, it is masked under the guise of a joke ("What?? I was just kidding!") or the insinuation that you are the problem ("Why are you so sensitive? Chill out, it's not that serious.")

Other times, you are made to feel like you don't have to do anything you don't want to do, but in reality, they are bossy, want to control your every move, and do not take your opinions seriously.

Your feelings and thoughts are valid, even when they don't entirely make sense to you. If someone in your circle belittles you, makes fun of your emotions, or acts like what you say doesn't matter, that is never okay.

You always feel drained or stressed after spending time with the person

Relationships can act like a battery in our lives—some fill us with energy and make us feel replenished. In contrast, others drain us and leave us feeling mentally or physically exhausted.

Begin to take notice of how you feel in the different relationships that you are in. If every time you hang out with someone in particular, you feel like they're sucking the energy out of you or you're mentally exhausted, that's a red flag that this is perhaps not a healthy relationship for you. And while no relationship is perfect, healthy relationships generally leave you feeling better, not worse, after an interaction.

So remember...

- "No" is a complete sentence in and of itself.

- Saying "no" does not make you a bad person.

- Saying "no" doesn't mean you're rude or unfriendly. It means you're strong, aware, and in control of your life.

- You have the right to put your safety and feelings first.

- When you set healthy limitations and learn to define what you will and will not do for yourself, you'll have more energy to invest in the things that mean the most to you.

- When we take care of ourselves and preserve the beauty of those things, we show up as better friends, sisters, brothers, and to anyone we care about.

- Love is always respectful. Always remember that you deserve to be treated with respect and kindness.

Internet and Social Media Safety

The internet is such a contradiction. On the one hand, it's great because it provides a quick and affordable opportunity to learn about the world around us, different cultures, and how other people live and think. It's an excellent place for us to join in and be a part of impactful movements and fight for the causes that we're passionate about. It has also become a popular channel to leverage our talents and make an extra income for ourselves.

On the other hand, the internet has made it much easier for malicious people to access personal information that can be used to harm, coerce, or bully you. When it comes to technology, the amazing possibilities seem endless, but the other side of it is just as dark. Despite all the good that comes with it, the internet is also where predators lurk to take advantage of young people like yourself.

Being safe online is also about protecting your personal data and information. We all know that there are a lot of scammers out there, so here are some things you should consider to ensure that you are safe online while enjoying the many benefits social media offers.

Once something is on the internet, it's there for good. You can say whatever you want on your online threads or social media timelines, but when doing so, keep in mind those prospective colleges or internships that you wish to apply to at some stage in your life because its success might depend upon what that prospective employer finds out about you online.

For example, suppose those recruiters or representatives were to find something about you online that does not reflect well on you as a candidate for their program or company. A situation like that may result in you getting overlooked for that opportunity, and you may never even know why you were overlooked in the first place.

Nothing ever truly gets "deleted" once it is posted online. Things like server storage, clouds, caches, archival sites, redistribution of your images or content by someone who has copied them, and even legal requirements make it virtually impossible for any data to be deleted, so your unwanted or regrettable post may still appear elsewhere.

Make your social accounts private. Is it just close families and friends that you want to see your online status? Decide for yourself and set your profile accordingly. You don't have to share everything on your social media profiles; you also have the power to be selective with who gets to glimpse your life.

Be mindful of what you share. Even with the strongest privacy settings, the internet isn't as private as we think. So, please think twice about what you are about to share. My go-to question is: *Is this something that I would feel okay with Grandma, Mom, or Dad seeing?* If your answer is no, think twice before posting.

Block those people who are bothering you. Is someone constantly sliding into your DMs or leaving inappropriate comments on your posts? Go to the settings tab and block them from interacting with your account. The best part about the block feature on social media is that they won't be notified.

Don't click on any suspicious "likes." Scammers and hackers are masters of disguise. These short messages, with URLs in the beginning, are often used as a guise to steal your personal information or for hackers to hack your accounts.

Encountering Sexual Predators

I hate to have to say this, but the truth is that there are people out there who prey on teens, and you must be aware of what you can do to protect yourself from falling into their trap. **We refer to young adults and older adults who do this as "predators."** Some predators will be obvious and explicit when trying to lure you into their dangerous web, but most are patient, subtle, and, more often than not, are not complete strangers. They are cunning and will try to manipulate you into thinking they are a "safe" person to be around.

Predators are especially dangerous because it doesn't matter how smart you are or how well your parents may have taught you about "stranger danger." They are willing to be patient and take all the time they need to befriend you and get you to trust them so that you feel safe sharing your most intimate thoughts. They are not always easy to spot because, unfortunately, most predators are people we already know.

The most important thing for you to know about predators is that they will always try to normalize inappropriate behavior. This is a process called "grooming," and often, our brains give us all kinds of red flags when this happens, but we often ignore these warning signals. And why do we ignore them? There are several reasons, but the most common ones are because we have grown to trust this person and don't want to make them feel "bad" or uncomfortable. We rationalize that they are "nice" or "harmless," even when some things they do or say make us uncomfortable. It has nothing to do with you being intelligent or clever! Predators are master manipulators who work hard to become great actors and fool everyone, even parents.

The "groom" or grooming process is when an adult normalizes inappropriate behavior between you and them. For example, they might give you compliments about your body or what they like/are attracted to. They might tell you to keep that relationship between you and them a secret because others would not approve. Or they start giving you expensive gifts unexpectedly.

The most dangerous part about the grooming process is that these behaviors are often done in plain sight. This means that they may say or do things in front of your friends or family members because they know that people will rarely call them out or confront them.

Predators can show up in many forms, but for the purposes of this chapter, I've put together a list of specific behaviors that signal you may be dealing with a sexual predator:

- **Overly Attentive.** Sexual predators are very attentive to you in those initial stages of your "relationship." They will respond to your text messages and calls in ways that seem innocent and harmless. This is how they get unsuspecting teens to become dependent on them. This is also the beginning of the grooming process.

- **They start taking an unusual interest in your life.** It feels nice to have someone give you a whole lot of attention, but when it seemingly comes out from nowhere, that's something that you should be suspicious of. Groomers try to do anything to make it seem like they are your friends and harmless. It's a way of manipulating you; sooner or later, they will ask for something in return.

- **They make mention of inappropriate topics with you.** They may start discussing their relationships and home life or even talk to you about their sex lives. They'll call you to have you as their shoulder to cry on. That is simply 100% wrong on all levels. You are not responsible for the emotional needs of any adult and should not be made to feel that you are the answer to them feeling better. Not ever!

- **They will try to spend time with you all alone.** Eventually, a groomer will attempt to have you spend time with them alone. This is so that they can tell you and say things to you that they would never say in the presence of others. It also allows them to get to know you and your likes/dislikes more and determine how easy it may be to manipulate you into doing their will. Remember, regardless of how kind, friendly, and sweet an adult seems to be, it's not normal for a grown adult to want to spend a lot of time with you alone or to do things such as offer you alcohol, weed, or any type of substance that might leave you unaware of your surroundings.

- **They will use gaslighting tactics to guilt-trip you into doing something.** Gaslighting is when someone uses psychological tactics to deny you of your reality. They lie to you or twist information to make it seem like you're overreacting or try to make you feel that you are a terrible person. They will try to make it known that you are being "unreasonable" or "unfair" to them, that all that they have been to you is a good person, and that they don't deserve the kind of treatment you are giving them right now. **Gaslighting can sound like any variation of the following:**

  - You're overreacting; that's really not a big deal.

  - Umm, no, that's not what happened... it didn't happen like that.

  - You should stop being so sensitive.

  - You are imagining things/ making stuff up.

  - Stop being so dramatic and overreacting over nothing.

  - I did not do that. You are the one who is lying.

  - Stop putting words in my mouth.

  - Omg, seriously? I was literally only joking! You need to relax.

- You don't really feel that way, do you? Nah, I don't think so.

- **They normalize secrecy and behaviors that are wrong.** For example, they will try to convince you to lie so that you can spend time with them. Or they'll force you to keep your interactions secret because they don't want anyone else to discover the inappropriate and illegal relationship they are trying to build. The secrecy makes it easier for them to continue with their psychological and, eventually, sexual abuse.

- **They exhibit jealousy.** They will easily get upset over spending time with your other friends or if you don't respond quickly enough to their texts. They want to keep tabs on your social accounts and private life. Sexual predators usually begin by trying to make you feel like you are the most important person in the world to them and then slowly begin to make you feel that you are devalued by others. This is done so that you begin to see them as the only person who truly cares about you.

- **They spend a whole lot of time around children or teens.** Most sexual predators rarely have friends their own age. And in those interactions, they will act inappropriately most of the time as well. They will kiss, hug, touch, or speak to the child or teen, even when they can see they are uncomfortable.

- **Sexual predators don't have a specific look or aesthetic about them.** Sometimes, it's a person who is as close to you as the family is. It can be the little league coach, the bus driver, the neighbor, a community leader, a family member, or the friend who's been like a part of your family for years. They can also be catfishers who pretend to be someone else as they gather information from you online.

Here are a final few pointers to help you protect yourself from those sexual predators lurking around.

- **Be careful who you talk to online.** If you start talking to someone online and they ask you to send them inappropriate pictures of yourself, don't do it under any circumstances and speak to someone you trust, preferably an adult who can help you if necessary. Don't ever give out your personal information to anyone unless you know for sure that it is for a verified and legitimate purpose that has been vetted by your parent or guardian.

- **Speak up.** If you find yourself in a situation you feel will go south very quickly, tell a friend, your mom, your dad, and your aunt—anyone you trust. By speaking up, you are letting that predator know that you are not an easy target. You will fight back and not tolerate or fall victim to their tactics.

- **Listen to that gut feeling.** That gut feeling doesn't lie. I am so grateful that this was reinforced to me from a young age. If you find yourself in a situation that doesn't feel right or is slightly off, don't be afraid to walk away. Rather be safe than sorry, right?

There is nothing wrong with you if you react to behavior that you find inappropriate, makes you feel uncomfortable, or is emotionally harmful. In healthy interactions, everyone has a place to speak up respectfully for themselves and expect empathy from the other person.

Street Smarts Safety Skills

Street safety or "street smarts" is a kind of intelligence that has nothing to do with the intelligence measured by test scores. It's all about how well you can read other people and how aware you are of your environment.

Being street-smart is a trait that will contribute to keeping you safe. When you're walking down the street or in a busy environment, it can be helpful to be alert to what is happening around you. Does the person walking towards you look particularly dangerous or dodgy? Is the person behind you walking at an oddly quick pace that is making you uncomfortable?

Suppose you figure out that the guy walking behind you is following you. You get that lightbulb moment and realize it might be safer to walk into a nearby shop or find a group of people you pretend to know and tell them you're being followed, then quickly dash into the safety of the next shop or restaurant you encounter. Being street-smart means being open and willing to learn in an environment far beyond the classroom.

Tips for Becoming More Street Smart

Learn to be vigilant. To be vigilant means to be watchful of your surroundings, alert to the happenings in your environment, and take reasonable precautions. **Being vigilant heightens your awareness and allows you to move forward cautiously, but it does not stop you from enjoying life.** Being paranoid comes with excessive or irrational suspicions without any real basis. Practice being vigilant by using your intuition and rationale to guide you along the way.

Stay with your friends. If you visit somewhere new that you've never been to, take a friend with you. People can often spot you if you need clarification about where you're going. So, if you have a friend with you, you are less likely to be a target.

Be alert when walking in public spaces. Avoid texting while walking because this will completely distract you from your surroundings. If you have your earphones in, ensure the volume is low enough to let you hear if something happens around you. Paying attention to your surroundings will help keep you safe and protect you from potential dangers.

Don't be afraid to use your voice. If you are in a public space and someone is making you feel all sorts of weird or scared, don't be afraid to scream or ask for help.

I remember this one time when I was still a college student, walking all alone back home, I noticed this group of guys following me. At first, I tried to tell myself that I was exaggerating, but suddenly, I said to myself, *"NOPE, YOU NEED TO LISTEN TO THE ALARM BELLS GOING OFF IN YOUR HEAD!"* I was uncomfortable about the whole situation and decided to move on to a more visible part of the street. I also decided to stop in at a restaurant and asked the hostess if I could wait there for a few minutes because there was a group of guys behind me that I didn't feel comfortable with. Did I care what they thought about my move to the other side of the street? Did I feel embarrassed to ask the hostess for some help? No way! As long as I was safe, that's all that mattered.

Keep your valuables stashed away. You might love wearing that cool ring that you got on your birthday, or you might also love showing off your latest MacBook, but if you aren't at all sure about the safety of the area that you're in, then it would be best for you to keep the stuff in your bag or pockets. If you have a backpack, ensure the straps are tightly around your shoulders to prevent someone from grabbing it while walking.

Know your whereabouts. If you are going to a new and unfamiliar place, the things that you should know include the whereabouts of the nearest police station. Are there places you can turn to if you run into trouble? Where are the emergency exits? This sounds over the top, but if you were to find yourself in an emergency such as this, you would be glad and grateful that you took the time to do the research.

Think and plan ahead. Plan your safety ahead of time. Back in college, I had a part-time job that involved me working many late nights. Before getting used to the neighborhood, I always mapped out the safest, best-lit route back home, and whenever possible, I tried to arrange for a friend to walk with me or meet me somewhere. That small amount of preparation gave me the boost I needed to walk around looking confident instead of looking like a lost lamb.

Always tell your parents, your caregivers, or a friend your whereabouts. If you have a phone, I recommend saving those important contacts in your "favorites" so you can easily reach them in an emergency.

There is only one of you, and you are irreplaceable. Your life is precious, so take good care of yourself and make your safety a priority. It's not about living a life constantly in fear; it's about a healthy level of common sense and protecting yourself from potential dangers.

Practical Safety Skills

Tim and his family are an adventurous bunch. They love being outdoors and are even bigger fans of camping. They are lucky enough to live near a camping facility, so he and his family take one weekend away each month to enjoy the sweet gifts that Mother Nature has to offer. Before a camping trip, Tim's parents always go through the safety precautions and procedures.

As Tim got older, he constantly thought, "Well, this is getting old. I don't see why we even have to go over these safety procedures every time we come out.. ugh." One day, he found himself on the camping site with a fire that had broken loose, and man, oh man, at that moment, he was so relieved that he'd spent all those hours sitting and listening through his parents' safety drills.

Creating A Family Safety Plan

A home safety plan isn't something that most families think about, and the thought of where to even begin can be overwhelming. Still, a home safety plan will help you determine what to do or who to call in case of an emergency situation. So, here are a few savvy tips that you can use now and for the rest of your life to create a safe and sound home for you. Start with creating a go-to family safety plan so that you are better prepared about what to do in an emergency.

Fire:

1. Figure out your escape routes in case a fire breaks out.

2. Ensure you and your family practice the entire drill at least three times a year.

3. If you stay in a double-story house, ensure you have a ladder that will act as an alternate escape route.

Natural Disaster:

1. Are there designated "safe areas" or spaces in the home in case of a natural disaster? Identify those together.

2. Determine where you're all going to meet. Pick a safe meeting point where everyone will try to gather.

Burglars:

You can't control whether or not a burglar will break into your house, but you can take steps and active measures to prevent a break-in. Here are some ideas for your family to consider:

- Install a sturdy deadbolt lock installed on doors that lead to the outside.

- Motions-sensing flood lights can be installed in the back and front yards. Have timers that automatically turn the lights on and off at certain hours. These will be a great deterrent for any unwanted guest wanting to invade your home.

- If you'll be leaving your home for a few days or longer, arrange for someone to care for the house, like a house-sitter, or arrange for the gardener to come and work in the garden during the daytime.

- Don't hide the spare keys under the carpet at the front door or in the pot plant by the entrance. Thieves know all those hiding places; instead, give the key to your neighbor or a trusted friend.

When you leave, make sure that the doors are always locked. In another universe, in a perfect world, we'd all have the liberty of leaving our doors wide open without the fear that anyone could just barge in and come and harm us. But sadly, the world we live in is a lot different from the vision we may have. Your home is meant to be your place of peace, so to ensure that you and the rest of the family have as much peace of mind as possible, make sure that the doors are closed and locked. Especially when Mom, Dad, or your caretaker are not around.

Practical Safety Tips For Home

If you spill something on the floor, wipe it immediately. An accident caused by a wet area can lead to severe medical emergencies. For example, you or one of your siblings might slip on that small amount of juice, break their arm, or fall and hit their head hard on the floor. It's scary stuff to mention or even think about, but we need to be aware that such things happen so that we don't become careless in the future.

Be extra cautious with flammable liquids. Keep flammable liquids, such as cleaning chemicals, away from fire sources, especially if you use a gas stove.

Ensure that medicine or pills are stored in spaces your younger siblings can't reach. Tiny humans will put just about anything in their mouths if it fits. And having pills lying around in random places is hazardous.

Make sure that the safety lights are turned on in the evening. Intruders are drawn to the dark. When the lights are off, they immediately think no one is around.

First Aid and Response Skills

Besides keeping yourself safe, there are a couple of other handy safety tips and tricks that will come in handy. I remember that first time I saw someone getting saved from choking on a french fry—yes, it was a french fry—with the Heimlich maneuver. Woah! I started to pay more attention during those first-aid lessons. Here are a couple of useful first-aid basics that you should know that will potentially help you save a life.

Remember your three P's. When you find yourself in a life-or-death situation, it can be pretty easy to let your emotions get the best of you and give in to the panic. But the three most important things that first aid is about are *preserving* life, *preventing* further injury, and helping the *patient* with recovery. These three P's serve as a reminder to do what you can with what you have in the safest way possible.

Inspect the surroundings for any further danger. You don't want to find yourself in a position where you, too, get injured. For example, if you find yourself in a situation where you have to help someone from a storm or heavy winds, before you jump in and help the person, try to make sure that there are no other immediate dangers lurking around, such as pieces of metal or glass being flung around by the wind. Once you have assessed the gravity of the situation, use your best judgment to create a strategy for how you will help without injuring yourself.

Treating cuts. If ever you're in a situation where you need to treat for cuts, you want to ensure that the person loses the least amount of blood possible. Look for a clean bandage; if you can't find one, a clean piece of cloth will do. Use it to apply pressure to the wound. If possible, attempt to clean the wound by running some clean water over it, applying some antiseptic or an antibiotic, and then covering the wound with a bandage.

Burn wounds. Before attempting to treat a **burn wound**, you will need to assess its severity. Major burns will require the assistance of a trained medical professional, so don't apply any ointments or moisturizers as they may further cause damage to the person's skin. Make sure you call 911 for assistance. The following information is provided so that you can know what to look out for in a burn victim:

- **First-degree burns: These types of burns affect the outer layer of the skin.** The skin would have a look that is similar to a sunburn. When dealing with minor burn wounds, you don't typically need to treat them extensively, but you could consider doing the following:

  o Running cool water over the burn wound.

  o Leave blisters as they are. Don't try to pop them.

  o Keep the burn wound out of direct sunlight.

- **Second-degree burns:** Some of the skin beneath the outer layer gets affected. Look for blisters that symbolize that a very painful kind of burn has taken place.

- **Third-degree burns:** Burns the entire inner layer of skin. Third-degree burn wounds will typically have a white or brownish color.

- **Fourth-degree burns:** These are burn wounds that penetrate the tissue all the way up to the tendons and bones.

Allergic reactions. Ever see a person's face puff up like a blowfish, have shortness of breath, or have an explosion of hives because they touched something they are hypersensitive to? That is a moderate to severe allergic reaction, and if not dealt with correctly and immediately, it can be life-threatening.

Here are a few things that may be helpful in this situation:

- Always call 911 first to get medical help for the person. Try to keep the person as calm as possible. Ask if they have an EpiPen with them.

- If they have an EpiPen and have indicated that they need help getting the shot, help them administer it.

- If the person is wearing a tie or tight clothing, loosen them so they can breathe much more quickly.

- Do not give them any food or medicine.

Prepping Your First Aid Kit

Everybody needs a first aid kit, at least I think so! You don't require professional medical training, just a few supplies that can help you out of many emergency situations. If you want to create your own first aid kit, this list is a basic starting point for what you'll need:

- Tourniquet

- Antiseptic/ antibacterial wipes

- Rubbing Alcohol

- Sunscreen

- Sling

- Burn-relief gel

- Gauze pads

- Scissors

Think About It...

How do you feel about all that you have learned in this chapter? It is a lot of information, but you can always return to these if you need a refresher. Before we move forward to our last chapter, let's look at a couple of questions that will help you reflect on everything you've learned in this chapter.

1. What is one rule for staying safe online? (Hint: it is about sharing personal information)

2. What are grooming behaviors that you should always be aware of?

3. Take a walk around your home and look for safety hazards. Were you able to find any?

4. What is your family's safety plan? If you don't have one, get together and agree on one together.

MY THOUGHTS

CHAPTER 8

Basic Daily Skills For A More Independent You

I've done a good amount of talking about some of the unexpected stuff and emotions that arise during your teen years. We've also covered some important personal and practical safety skills that will help keep you safe. In this final Chapter, I would like to take you on a detour from all that and talk about some skills you can learn to start feeling more independent and grown up.

Have you ever wondered how amazing it would feel to fix your bike, create a mouthwatering meal, or even save enough cash for those trendy, overly-priced sneakers you've wanted or even your dream car?

Sounds both thrilling and nerve-wracking, right? By learning some of the skills I'm about to talk to you about, all this and more can become your reality. These skills won't just impress your friends and family; they're also your ticket to self-reliance, creative problem-solving, and a sense of accomplishment like no other.

Time Management Skills: Manage Your Time Like A Pro!

Don't tell my daughter that I told you, but towards the end of middle school, I was beginning to seriously worry about her time management skills. Eighth grade was particularly challenging. If she wasn't frantically running out of the house in the morning gathering her things, she would be panicking because she forgot to do something for school that could've been done earlier. As I write these lines, I'm happy to report that she's made a considerable change and has *mostly* figured out how to optimally manage her time. This change allows her time to indulge in the things that bring her joy, like playing sports or hanging out with her friends and family.

Time management skills are beneficial not only in your personal life but also in your professional life. One day, when you're out at work, your time management skills will show your employers, clients, or patients that you are trustworthy and reliable. If you don't find a way to manage your time, you'll most likely find yourself stressed and overwhelmed when your workload feels like it's impossible to manage.

There are a ton of time management tools, productivity gadgets, calendars, and types of to-do lists on cool online boards. But what I have found with time management is that simple and practical works better when you want to lead a more productive and efficient lifestyle.

Prioritize and organize accordingly. Schedule your tasks based on what's important and urgent right now. If you have an assignment due the following day, you will want to prioritize that over a two-hour run of your favorite TV show. Ask yourself this golden question: *"In terms of importance, can this wait until tomorrow?"* If you answer yes, it's probably **not** the most urgent thing on your to-do list.

- **Put it in your calendar and plan ahead.** Take a day of the week, like Sunday, to map out how you will tackle the week. Schedule your "focus time" into your calendar or agenda in the same manner as you would any high-priority task.

- **Remove all distractions.** This means turning your phone on airplane mode or do not disturb mode. Closing all tabs on your browser that are not pertinent to the task at hand. Not checking social media, texts or emails when focusing on what you are doing.

- **Do similar tasks together.** This will help you stay more focused and reduce the possibility of losing focus to a different task.

- **Time yourself.** Set timers when you're busy with tasks to determine how much time you want to spend on them. Whether it is 30 minutes, 60 minutes or 90 minutes, set your timer accordingly.

- **Rest in between long sessions of work.** It's easy to think that you will get more done if you work for long periods, but without a break, that may actually decrease your productivity. Everyone's attention span is different. If you aren't sure how long you will be able to focus on something before needing a break, start with 25 minutes of focus and then give yourself a 5-minute break before returning to the task.

- **Be realistic.** If you already know that you will have a busier week, you don't have to expect yourself to do more. That's a recipe for burnout! You want to ensure that the workload is still manageable, and this sometimes means moving things around in your schedule or canceling non-priority things.

Money Matters- It's Never Too Early To Budget and Save

Marcus' Money Mishap

I have one last teen who I would like you to meet. His name is Marcus, and he is a savvy young man. Marcus has big hopes and dreams and is always looking for simple ways to help him prepare for the future that awaits him. Just recently, one of his closest friends, Gabriel, came to school with the biggest smile. *"Bro!"* Gabriel greeted him with infectious and palpable excitement. *"I just got my own bank account this weekend and made my first deposit!"* he said, whipping out his new bank card.

Marcus was impressed. *"That's so slick. You know, I've been wanting to do that too so that I don't have to give my checks from work to my mom to deposit in her account. Know what? I'mma ask Mom if I can get my own account too."*

When that afternoon bell rang, signaling the end of the school day, Marcus bolted for the door and headed home. *"Hey, Mom, I'm home! Guess what? Gabriel just got his own bank account with money he got for his birthday! Can I open a bank account when I turn sixteen next month? I always get money from Uncle John for my birthday, so I could use that to start it."*

At first, Marcus' mother looked at him curiously, then gleefully responded: *"Oh, honey, don't worry about all that. You're way too young to worry about money. You can figure all that out when you're older. If you need money, just ask me."*

Even though he knew his mother had good intentions, her response frustrated Marcus beyond words. He felt stuck because he thought her feelings would be hurt if he insisted on opening his bank account. So, instead of explaining to his mom that he really wanted to learn how to manage his own money and make deposits into his own account, he smiled, agreed with her, and walked away with the assumption that talking about money was not open to discussion.

Still, Marcus was curious and wanted to save for a new PlayStation. He knew he would be more motivated to save by learning how to budget and watching his money grow, so he searched online and researched ways to save money without a bank account. Marcus found a lot of good information, but only some things made sense. Man, oh man, did he wish his mother was helping him through this first financial journey.

Learning to budget is a life skill that will teach you to become the kind of adult who is financially responsible and doesn't make impulsive financial decisions. Understanding the value of money at this early age will help you think more thoughtfully about how you spend it.

Ways For Teens To Earn Money

You've got a lot on your plate: school, after-school and weekend activities, homework, and a social life to manage. If you can find time to work, it will likely be very part-time. Still, there are ways that you can earn some extra pocket money for yourself:

- **Babysitting.** If you like taking care of younger kids, this can be a great way of making spending money during the weekends.

- **Lifeguarding.** This is a great summer job for those of you who are excellent swimmers and are willing to learn how to be a lifeguard. Lifeguard jobs are available in many places: private and public pools, beaches, waterparks, state parks, and more!

- **Tutoring.** Enjoy teaching? You might find some excellent income opportunities by becoming a tutor for younger students. You can become a tutor in many different areas, ranging from math and reading to writing and more. The possibilities are endless! Tutors can also find work that will fit their schedules, ranging from one-on-one work to working at learning centers in a group setting.

- **Helping out the neighbors.** No matter what type of setting you live in, everybody needs help with something. Your neighbors may need help with dog walking, yard work, snow removal, or even going food shopping for them. You can start by asking your parents or their friends what they might need help with and see if it is something that you can help with.

- **Cashier.** Most of our local stores have at least one or two teens employed on a part-time basis at any given time throughout the year. An application can be made online for many of these positions.

- **Sell stuff you own that is no longer wanted or needed.** This can be anything from clothing to old toys to birthday gifts that never got opened or used. This may require some shipping and setting up of accounts, so remember to enlist the help of a trusted adult.

You can make money in multiple ways but remember that saving some of it is just as important. Saving isn't easy when there are so many cool things that you could buy with all that money, right? Here's the thing: if you save well now, you'll be so much prouder of yourself when you finally get to that point when you can buy yourself that thing you have been dreaming about for ages. Here are a few of my favorite and savviest saving tips to get you started.

- **Create a budget.** Having a budget will help you determine where your money comes from and where you are spending. Start with a two-column worksheet: One column is marked as "INCOME" (money in) and the other column marked as "EXPENSES" (money out). Your income might be your allowance or money from your student job. Expenses might be things like shopping, outings, or clothing. Keep your receipts until you log them into the "expenses" column. If columns aren't your thing, many free budgeting apps are available for teens—check out your app store!

- **Cut back on spending.** Instead of buying lunch, consider bringing your own lunch. If you love clothing, instead of heading for name brands, check out "no-name" brands that still give you the look you want. If you want to find hidden gems, check out secondhand shops!

Saving money can be a fun and empowering experience, and you are never too young to start doing it. If you begin the habit of putting money into savings now, you're more likely to continue to do so when you become an adult, which will benefit you big-time in the long run.

Become a Mini-Chef Overnight!

I know this may be hard to believe, but cooking is not that difficult. It's one of the most straightforward skills you can learn, and if you know how to do it properly, believe me when I say that you will save yourself a lot of money. So, let's get to it and teach you some basics about how to get around in the kitchen.

- **Hygiene always comes first.** We come into contact with many surfaces throughout the day, so to prevent spreading germs or cross-contamination, ensure you wash your hands before touching the food you cook!

- **Be cautious of knives.** When it comes to the kitchen, a blunt knife can be more dangerous than a sharp knife. So, always make sure you use a sharp knife and never leave your knives lying around on the edge of the countertop.

- **Be sure to switch off all appliances when you're finished using them.** We don't want any accidents or fires breaking out!

- **Clean up after yourself.** I use the "clean as you go" method, which means I throw stuff out if I don't need it, put stuff away in the cabinets or refrigerator when I'm done with them and wipe down any spills. It makes the post-meal clean-up so much easier!

Easy Recipes at Your Fingertips

You might not always have time (or the skills) to whip up a five-course meal for yourself, but just because you don't have the time doesn't mean you can't make a decent meal. I will share three of the easiest, most delicious recipes that are still my go-to when I don't have much time (or someone around to do it for me). Enjoy!!

Cheesiest Grilled Cheese Toasted Sandwich

What You'll Need

- Fresh bread: white, brown bread, sourdough—whichever kind you enjoy will work perfectly.
- Mayonnaise: will help a lot with maintaining that crisp exterior of the bread.
- Dijon mustard: to add a nice tang to the sandwich
- Butter
- Cheese: preferably cheddar. If you have two types, such as mozzarella and cheddar, even better!

Method

1. Spread the mayo on the outside of the bread and the Dijon mustard on the inside of the bread
2. Add your grated cheese to the slices of bread
3. Turn your stove on to medium heat and add some butter to your pan until it coats the whole bottom
4. Add your bread and cover the skillet. Cook it for three to four minutes on each side until it's crisp and golden
5. When the bread is evenly browned on both sides, remove it from the heat, slice, and enjoy!

Scrambled Eggs on Toast

What you need

- Bread: sandwich bread will work perfectly.
- Eggs
- Cheese
- Butter to help add more flavor to your eggs.
- Salt and pepper to taste

Method

- Whisk your eggs, salt, and pepper together.
- Add your butter to a pan on medium heat. While it melts, you can start toasting your bread.
- Once the butter has melted, add your eggs. Slowly move the egg mixture around in the pan. You want your eggs to have a soft, custard consistency, so you'll most likely cook them for about two minutes.
- Add your cheese, and cook for an additional minute. Remove them from your heat and spoon the mixture over your toasted bread.

If you want to be a little fancy, top it off with some dried or fresh herbs and enjoy!

Pasta with Tomato Sauce

What You'll Need

- 2 tbsp of oil
- 1 diced onion
- 1 tin of chopped tomatoes or jarred tomato sauce
- 1 pinch of sugar
- Salt and pepper
- Dried or fresh basil
- 300g of pasta (any kind that you like)

Method

1. Heat the oil in the saucepan, and once warm, add your onions. Cook them at medium heat until they've browned or softened. In a separate pot, bring water to a boil.
2. Add the tomatoes, basil, pinch of salt, and sugar, cook for 10-15 more minutes, and stir until your sauce thickens.
3. While the sauce cooks, add your pasta to the other pot and cook it according to the package instructions or until it's al dante (soft but still resistant to the bite).
4. Drain the pasta water (reserve 3 tablespoons of it which you will use later), add the pasta to the sauce, add the 3 tablespoons of pasta water, and cook it for an additional 4–5 minutes.
5. Remove from the heat. Spoon onto plates. You can grate some parmesan or add some fresh basil as a garnish. And it's Bon Appetite for you!

Think About It...

Learning any of these skills may seem like a steep climb, but remember that every empowering journey begins with that first step, followed by another, and yet another until you've mastered each one. *I'm excited to see you on the road to increased self-confidence and independence...*

1. Think back to the recipe guide. Which meal sounds best to you? Try to make it!

2. Reflect on your cooking experience. How was the meal? What would you do differently next time?

3. What are three key things you can do right now to manage your time better?

4. Do you have any kind of budgeting system in place? If not, think about how you can start implementing one.

MY THOUGHTS

Final Pearls Of Wisdom

Starting anything new is always challenging, but that doesn't mean it's impossible! You might be sitting on the couch or on your bed thinking, *"Well, I've made it to the end of the book. Now what?"* **My advice to you is to start anywhere.** Do something small, like making your bed, ask your parents or guardians if you can help them with something, or start with a simple affirmation where you tell yourself, *"I've got this! I can do anything that I set my mind to."* We learn best when we immerse ourselves in experiences. In other words, go ahead and try!

Sure, you'll be imperfect and mess up, but that is the joy and curse of this thing we call "adulting." You don't have to rush through the process, either. Success is not always measured by a big, impactful outcome, and progress is sometimes slow, which is okay. You'll get there eventually, and when you do, you will be so proud of yourself for persevering. But for now, enjoy the ride and give yourself a pat on the back because the very fact that you made it to the end of this book means that you are much better informed than where you started.

Last but not least, I would like to leave you with some pearls of wisdom that have led me through very difficult times and always helped keep me grounded. I hope that they do the same for you:

* Aim for progress, not perfection, because perfection is rarely possible, but progress is always a possibility.

* Love and enjoy who you are today.

* Practice small bits of gratitude every day. It will help fight off sadness and remind you that even little things can bring you joy.

* A kind word can make a difference in someone's world. Be kind to yourself and to others.

* Instead of saying *"I'm not good at that"*, try saying *"I can learn to be better at that."*

* A "bad" grade does not define you. It is merely a moment in time.

* Know that you are loved, as you are, uniquely you.

Keep Going, Kid!

WAS THIS BOOK HELPFUL?

**If you enjoyed reading this book
and want to spread the word...**

Review this book and let your voice be heard.

Scan the QR code to submit your review!

☆☆☆☆☆

References

Abuse Lawsuit. (n.d.). *What Is Sexual Grooming? Signs To Spot An Abuser.*
https://www.abuselawsuit.com/resources/sexual-grooming/

Baker, W. (2021, November 20). *Scrambled eggs on toast.* Salt & Baker.
https://saltandbaker.com/scrambled-eggs-on-toast/

Berkeley Well-Being Institute. (n.d.). *How to get over disappointment: Examples and strategies.* The Berkeley Well-Being Institute.
https://www.berkeleywellbeing.com/disappointment.html

Berry, K. (2022, December 24). *Use This Chart to Know How often To Clean everything.* Housewife How-Tos.
https://housewifehowtos.com/clean/how-often-to-clean-things-in-your-home/

Better Health Channel. (2012). *Teenagers and communication.* Better Health.
https://www.betterhealth.vic.gov.au/health/healthyliving/teenagers-and-communication

Borges, A. (2020, May 21). *9 Therapist-Approved Tips for Managing All Your Feelings.* Self.
https://www.self.com/story/emotional-regulation-skills

Brooks, A. W., & John, L. K. (2018, May). *How to Ask Great Questions.* Harvard Business Review.
https://hbr.org/2018/05/the-surprising-power-of-questions

Byham, E. R. (2020, May 11). *The Abuser in the car.* The Personal Growth Project.
https://www.thepersonalgrowthproject.com/blog/the-abuser-in-the-car

Cascio, C. N., O'Donnell, M. B., Tinney, F. J., Lieberman, M. D., Taylor, S. E., Strecher, V.J., & Falk, E. B. (2016). *Self-affirmation activates brain systems associated with self-related processing and reward and is reinforced by future orientation. Social Cognitive and Affective Neuroscience, 11(4), 621-629.*

Cebollero, C. (2018, April 20). *Council Post: The Seven Key Steps Of Critical Thinking.* Forbes.
https://www.forbes.com/sites/forbescoachescouncil/2018/04/20/the-seven-key-steps-of-critical-thinking/

Chill Skills In a Jar: *Anger Management Tips for Teens.* (2021). Minneapolis: Free Spirit Publishing.

CNET. (2021, September 18). *How to Create a Home Safety Plan for Your Family*. CNET. https://www.cnet.com/home/security/how-to-create-a-home-safety-plan-for-your-family/

Cochrane, A. (2022, March 3). *How to Overcome a Negative Body Image*. SUU. https://www.suu.edu/blog/2022/03/overcome-negative-body-image.html

Contributor, F. Z. (2021, June 19). *A Psychologist Shares the 4 Styles of Parenting—and the Type that Researchers Say is the Most Successful*. CNBC. https://www.cnbc.com/2021/06/29/child-psychologist-explains-4-types-of-parenting-and-how-to-tell-which-is-right-for-you.html#:~:text=different%20paren

Cooks-Campbell, A. (2022, January 28). *Thinking Outside The box: 8 Ways to Become a Creative Problem Solver*. Better Up https://www.betterup.com/blog/thinking-outside-the-box

Wilson, T. D., & Schooler, J. W. (1991). Thinking too much: Introspection can reduce the quality of preferences and decisions. Journal of Personality and Social Psychology, 60(2), 181-192.

Eval Community. (n.d.). *What is Evaluation* https://www.evalcommunity.com/career-center/what-is-evaluation/

Ferriss, T. (2015, October 30). *How to Say No When It Matters Most (or "Why I'm Taking a Long 'Startup Vacation'")* The Blog of Author Tim Ferriss. https://tim.blog/2015/10/29/startup-vacation-2/

Gibson, J. (n.d.). *The Value of Street Smarts*. Linkedin https://www.linkedin.com/pulse/value-street-smarts-jerome-gibson

Gobet, F., & Simon, H. A. (1996). Templates in chess memory: A mechanism for recalling several boards. Cognitive Psychology, 31(1), 1-40.

Good Housekeeping. (2022, September 21). *How to Clean a Student House*. Good Housekeeping. https://www.goodhousekeeping.com/uk/house-and-home/household-advice a681733/essential-cleaning-tips-for-students/

Healithsta. (2019, January 25). *How to spot a sexual predator - the 8 characteristics - Healthista*. https://www.healthista.com/how-to-spot-a-sexual-predator-characteristics/

Hessel, E. T. (PhD). (2023, June). *Coping With Cliques*. KidsHealth. https://kidshealth.org/en/teens/cliques.html

Life Skills Advocate. (2021, December 16). *How To Teach Teens How To Ask For Help* Life Skills Advocate. https://lifeskillsadvocate.com/blog/how-to-teach-teens-to-ask-for-help/

LinkedIn. (2022, March 8). *What are Some effective Ways to Calm Your Nerves Before Speaking in public?* Linkedin https://www.linkedin.com/advice/o/what-some-effective-ways-calm-your-nevers-before

Melrose Alliance Against Violence. (2023). *Teen Dating Abuse.* MAAV. https://www.maav.org/get-educated/teen-dating-abuse/

Mathee, J. (2022, April 13). *Exercise for Teenagers: How Much They Need, and How to Fit It In.* Healthline. https://www.healthline.com/health/fitness/exercise-for-teenagers

Neff, K. D. (2003). *Self-compassion: An alternative conceptualization of a healthy attitude toward oneself. Self and Identity,* 2(2), 85-101.

Nelson, A. (2020). *Between screens and dreams: Exploring the sleep-FOMO connection in teens.* Pediatric Research, 87(1), 21-28.

Olive Magazine. (2022, September 1). *44 Student Recipes.* Olivemagazine. https://www.olivemagazine.com/recipes/collection/best-ever-easy-recipes-for-students/

Owens, J., & Adolescent Sleep Working Group. (2014). *Insufficient sleep in adolescents and young adults: An update on causes and consequences.* Pediatrics, 134(3), e921-e932

Padma. (2014, August 5). *6 Negative Effects Of Peer-Pressure.* The Teachers Digest. http://theteachersdigest.com/6-ways-in-which-children-are-negatively-affected-by-peer-pressure/

Pohl, J. C. (2017, August 27). *3 Ways to Teach Your Teen How to Overcome Disappointment.* TEEN TRUTH. https://teentruth.net/3-ways-teach-teen-overcome-disappointment/

Psychology Compass. (2020, January 24). *Contradict yourself to become more open-minded. Psychology* Compass. https://psychologycompass.com/blog/open-minded/

Rabbitt, M. (n.d.). *How to Help Kids Deal with Disappointment.* Parents. https://www.parents.com/toddlers-preschoolers/development/social/helping-kids-deal-with-disappointment/

Reigions. (n.d.). *Budgeting for Teens: Teaching Teens to Save*. RegionsBank. https://www.regions.com/insights/personal/personal-finances/budgeting-and-saving/teaching-teens-how-to-save-money

Robbins, M. (Host). (2023, September 14). Episode 101: Raw and Refreshing Advice on Navigating Anxiety, Popularity, Insecurity, and Peer Pressure in Your Teenage and 20-Something Years [Audio podcast episode]. *In The Mel Robbins Podcast with Oakley Robbins*.

Sagari Gongala. (2014, July 25). *21 Essential Life Skills For Teens To Learn*. MomJunction; https://www.momjunction.com/articles/everyday-life-skills-your-teen-should-learn_0081859/

Smith, J. D., & Johnson, L. R. (2019). *Nightly scrolls: The impact of FOMO on adolescent sleep patterns*. Journal of Adolescent Health, 54(2), 238-244.

Stay Safe. (n.d.). *Safety at Home: 10 Common Safety Hazards around the House* StaySafe.org. https://staysafe.org/safety-at-home-10-common-safety-hazards-around-the-house/

sy@dmin. (2022, January 18). *The Power of No: Why Saying "No" is Important* Synergy Health Programs. https://synergyhealthprograms.com/why-saying-no-is-important/

Tutor Doctor. (n.d.). *The Importance of Teaching Your Teens Life Skills*. Tutor Doctor. https://www.tutordoctor.co.uk/blog/2021/march/the-imporance-of-teaching-your-teens-life-skill/#:~:text=Learning%20life%20skills%20doesn

UCAS. (n.d.). *Ten Tips For Keeping Your Student Room Clean and Tidy*. UCAS. Accommodation.ucas.com. Retrieved April 14, 2023, from https://accommodation.ucas.com/article/ten-tips-keeping-your-room-clean

Unsplash. (2020, September 2). *Photo by Michael Jin* on Unsplash. Unsplash.com. https://unsplash.com/photos/8ICseEiNO0c

U.S. Department of Health and Human Services. (2018). *Current Guidelines*. https://health.gov/our-work/nutrition-physical-activity/physical-activity-guidelines/current-guidelines

Univer, E. (2018, February 2). *How to Take a Shower The Right Way*. Teen Vogue. https://www.teenvogue.com/story/best-showering-skincare-tips

Vann, M. R. (2013, April 3). *Skin Care For Teen Skin*. Everyday Health. https://www.everydayhealth.com/skin-and-beauty/skin-care-for-teen-skin.aspx

Wilson, T. D., & Schooler, J. W. (1991). Thinking too much: Introspection can reduce the quality of preferences and decisions. Journal of Personality and Social Psychology, 60(2), 181-192.

Wright, A. (2017, September 16). *You're Not Alone in This: 15 Hard Adulting Truths.* Annie Wright, LMFT. https://www.anniewright.com/youre-not-alone-in-this-15-hard-adulting-truths/

YCS. (2021, July 22). Importance of a clean bedroom. Yorleny's Cleaning Service, LLC. https://yorlenyscleaningservice.com/why-important-clean-bedroom-benefits/

Image References

Arnoldes, P. (2015). Scrambled eggs with various spices [Image]. Pexels. https://www.pexels.com/photo/scrambled-eggs-with-various-spices-6109498/

Dumlao, N. (2020). Grilled Cheese [Image]. In Unsplash. https://unsplash.com/photos/_wA_5FSU4NQ

Nelson, Z. (2017). Jumps [Image]. In Unsplash https://unsplash.com/photos/98Elr-LIvD8

Stuccio, C. (2019). Tomato Pasta [Image]. In Unsplash. https://unsplash.com/photos/2CZ0Zpuj-gU

Made in United States
Troutdale, OR
08/09/2024

21862723R00084